Early Bloomers

in Stained Glass

by Brenda Henning

Credits

Written and illustrated by Brenda Henning
Edited by Marcia Harmening
Models stitched by Virginia Benson
Photography by
Ken Wagner
1100 E Union, Seattle, WA 98122
(206)328-1030
Printed in the United States of America

Introduction

Flowers are an ever-present reminder of days past, and a fragrant promise for tomorrow.

ISBN 0-9648878-8-6

Bear Paw Productions
4015 Iona Circle
Anchorage, AK 99507
(907)349-7873

Table of Contents

Catalog

Write or call Bear Paw Productions for a complete list of currently available books and patterns by Brenda Henning.

Clover Quick Bias® also available from Bear Paw Productions in Black, Gold, Silver and Black Lamé.

Project Supply Lists

Daffodil

Fabric Requirements

Bias Tape
16 1/2 yards
(used 15 1/2 yards)

Background - 3/4 yard
Yellows - 1/2 yard assorted
ranging from light to
medium/dark
Greens - 3/8 yard assorted
Border - 3/8 yard
Backing - 3/4 yard
Binding - 1/2 yard
Woven Fusible Interfacing (optional) - 1 yard

Tulips

Fabric Requirements

Bias Tape
13 1/2 yards
(used 12 1/2 yards)

Background - 3/4 yard
Raspberry - 3/8 yard assorted
ranging from light to
medium/dark
Greens - 3/8 yard assorted
Border - 3/8 yard
Backing - 3/4 yard
Binding - 1/2 yard
Woven Fusible Interfacing (optional) - 1 yard

Pansies

Fabric Requirements

Bias Tape
14 1/2 yards
(used 13 1/2 yards)

Background - 3/4 yard
Yellow - 1/4 yard
Greens - 1/4 yard assorted
Purples - 1/4 yard assorted
Gold - 2" square
Border - 3/8 yard
Backing - 3/4 yard
Binding - 1/2 yard
Woven Fusible Interfacing (optional) - 1 yard

Hothouse Rose

Fabric Requirements

Bias Tape
13 1/2 yards
(used 12 1/2 yards)

Background - 3/4 yard
Pinks - 1/2 yard assorted
ranging from light to
medium/dark
Greens - 1/4 yard assorted
Border - 3/8 yard
Backing - 3/4 yard
Binding - 1/2 yard
Woven Fusible Interfacing (optional) - 1 yard

Other basic supplies needed for Quilt As You Go Stained Glass:

freezer paper
#60/8 sewing machine needles
Roxanne's Glue-Baste-It!®
masking tape
sewing awl
fine black thread or smoke nylon thread
cotton batting

Quilt As You Go Stained Glass

Fabric Selection

The fabrics chosen for use in the stained glass quilts are as follows:

Background	P & B Naturescapes
Borders	Hoffman Bali Batiks
Flowers	predominately Benartex Fossil Ferns
Greens	predominately Benartex Fossil Ferns

All fabrics listed above are current as this book goes to print. Unfortunately, fabrics are forever being discontinued and new ones introduced. When searching for the perfect fabric for use in your quilt, please contact your local quilting shop; they are your best source for current fabrics.

When selecting fabric for stained glass I look for tone-on-tone prints to use in the design areas. Solid fabrics have been used by many, but I believe that mottled prints give the illusion of actual stained glass windows.

The hand-dyed batik prints, used in the borders, act to bring all of the colors of the quilt together. The focus fabric unifies the quilt.

Fabric Preparation

Many students, over the years, have come to class with unwashed fabrics. Their reasoning is sound - "this quilt is going to be a wall hanging; I don't want to wash away the soil resistance of the fabric sizing!" Unfortunately, this logic does not apply to stained glass construction.

Prewash all fabrics to be used in this project! This removes the sizing that may prevent the fusible bias tape from adhering properly. Do not use spray starch either. Starch may also reduce the effectiveness of the fusible.

Foundation Preparation

The "foundation" used in this project will be the background fabric. The foundation serves as the base to which all other pieces of fabric are applied. The background fabric selected should be light in color. Medium and dark colored background fabrics will act to dull or gray the color of the fabrics applied to it, making your pretty flower fabric appear dirty.

•Press the background fabric. Do not use spray starch or sizing on either side of the background fabric as you press it.

•Cut the background fabric 23" x 34". This is slightly larger than the pattern. Due to printing limitations, the actual pattern size is 21 3/4" x 31 1/2". The design has been drawn with these limitations in mind.

•Center the background fabric, **right side up**, over the pattern and pin in place.

•Trace the entire design onto the right side of the background fabric using a #2 pencil or an Ultra Fine Point Sharpie permanent marking pen. Tape the pattern/fabric assembly to a large window if it is difficult to see the design well enough to trace.

Basting Appliqué Shapes

Freezer Paper Templates and Glue Basting

While a number of methods exist for securing the appliqué pieces to the background fabric, I have chosen glue basting for this project. This method lends itself well to the needs of those who would rather hand stitch the leading in place.

•Cut two 22" lengths of freezer paper and butt the 22" long edges. Splice the two pieces by placing **masking tape** on the paper (matte) side of the freezer paper. (Use masking tape - clear tape will melt when touched by an iron.) Trim to 22" x 33".

•Center the freezer paper, paper side up, over the pattern - pin or tape in place.

•Trace the entire design, **right side up**, onto the freezer paper using a #2 pencil or an Ultra Fine Point Sharpie.

•Trace the leading lines of the border pieces to the edge of the freezer paper. The **border** segments are treated just as you would any other appliqué unit.

•Cut the freezer paper exactly on the pencil lines with paper scissors.

•Adjacent pieces that are of the same fabric may be cut as one unit - such as leaf halves. Pay close attention to directional fabric. The resulting placement of a directional print may be undesirable.

•Press the shiny side of the freezer paper to the **right side** of the selected fabrics using a warm iron. Avoid overheating the freezer paper; it may cause the paper to be difficult to remove.

•Fabric grain lines are not important. Place freezer paper in such a way as to make the best use of a fabric design.

•Cut the fabric slightly larger than the adhered freezer paper - 1/16" extra will allow the fabric raw edges to overlap a little when basting the pieces to the background.

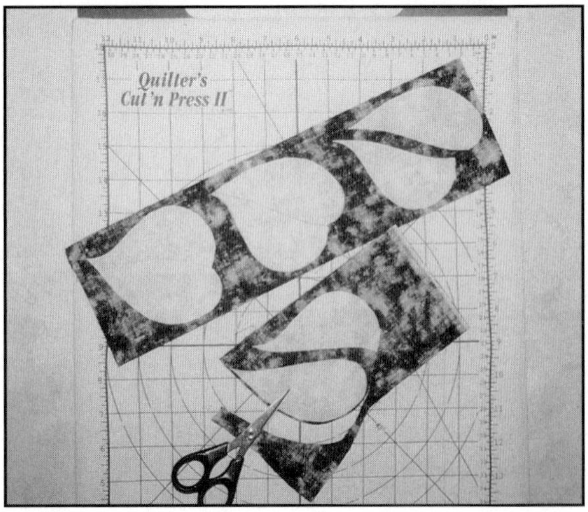

•Remove the freezer paper from the cut fabric section.

•Place dots of basting glue on the background fabric along the outline of the piece to be placed. Glue basting is diagramed below using **Roxanne's Glue-Baste-It!**

•Carefully position the fabric piece on the background fabric. All dots of glue should be covered by the applied fabric. Allow the glue to dry.

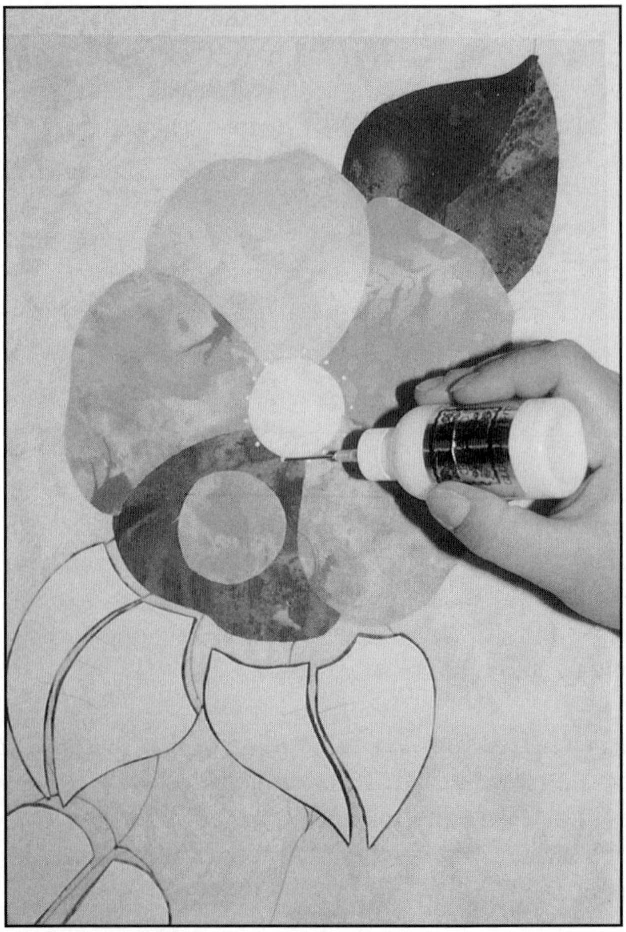

Hothouse Rose

Bear Paw Productions
4015 Iona Circle • Anchorage, AK 99507
(907)349-7873 • Phone & FAX

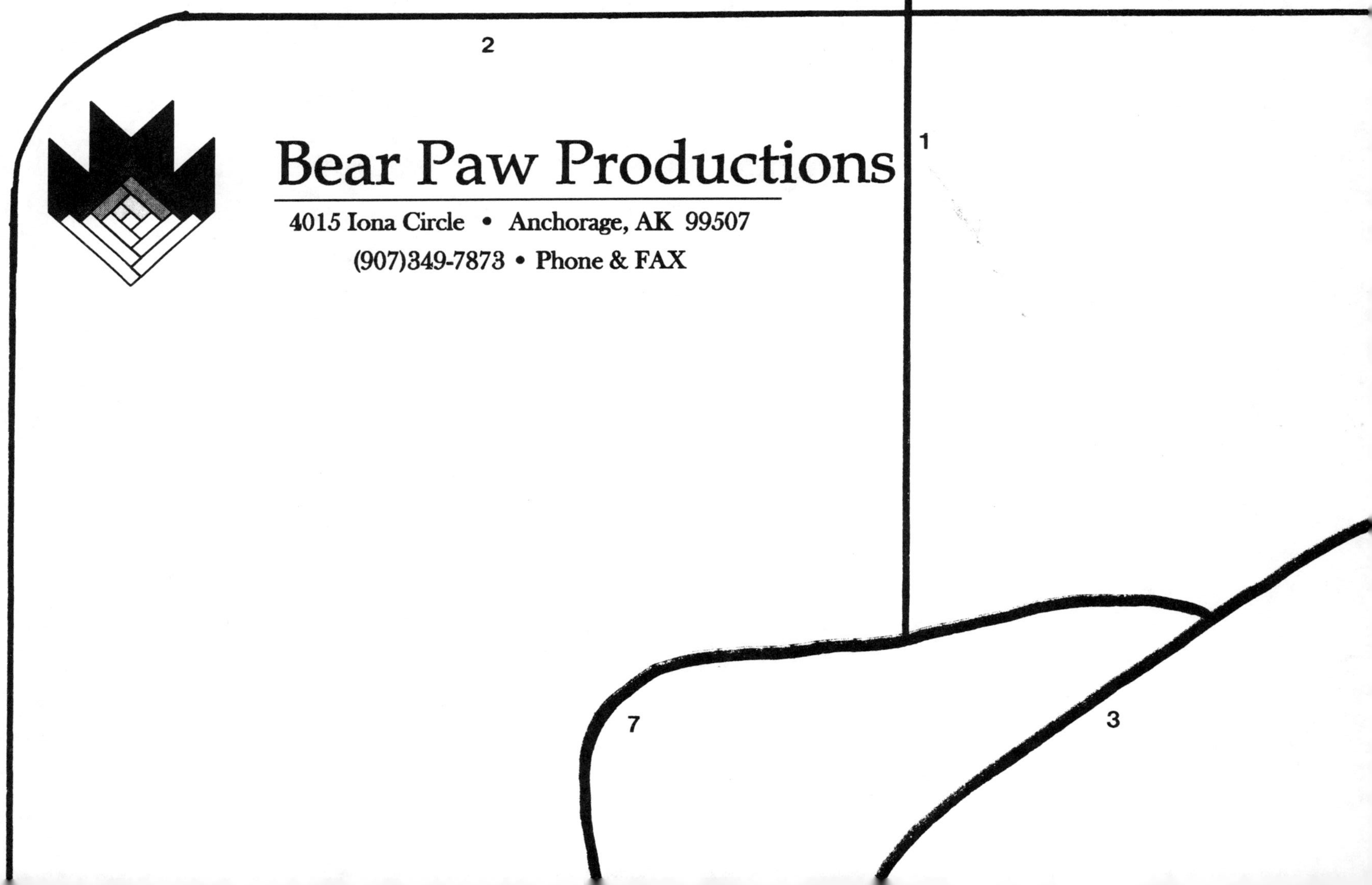

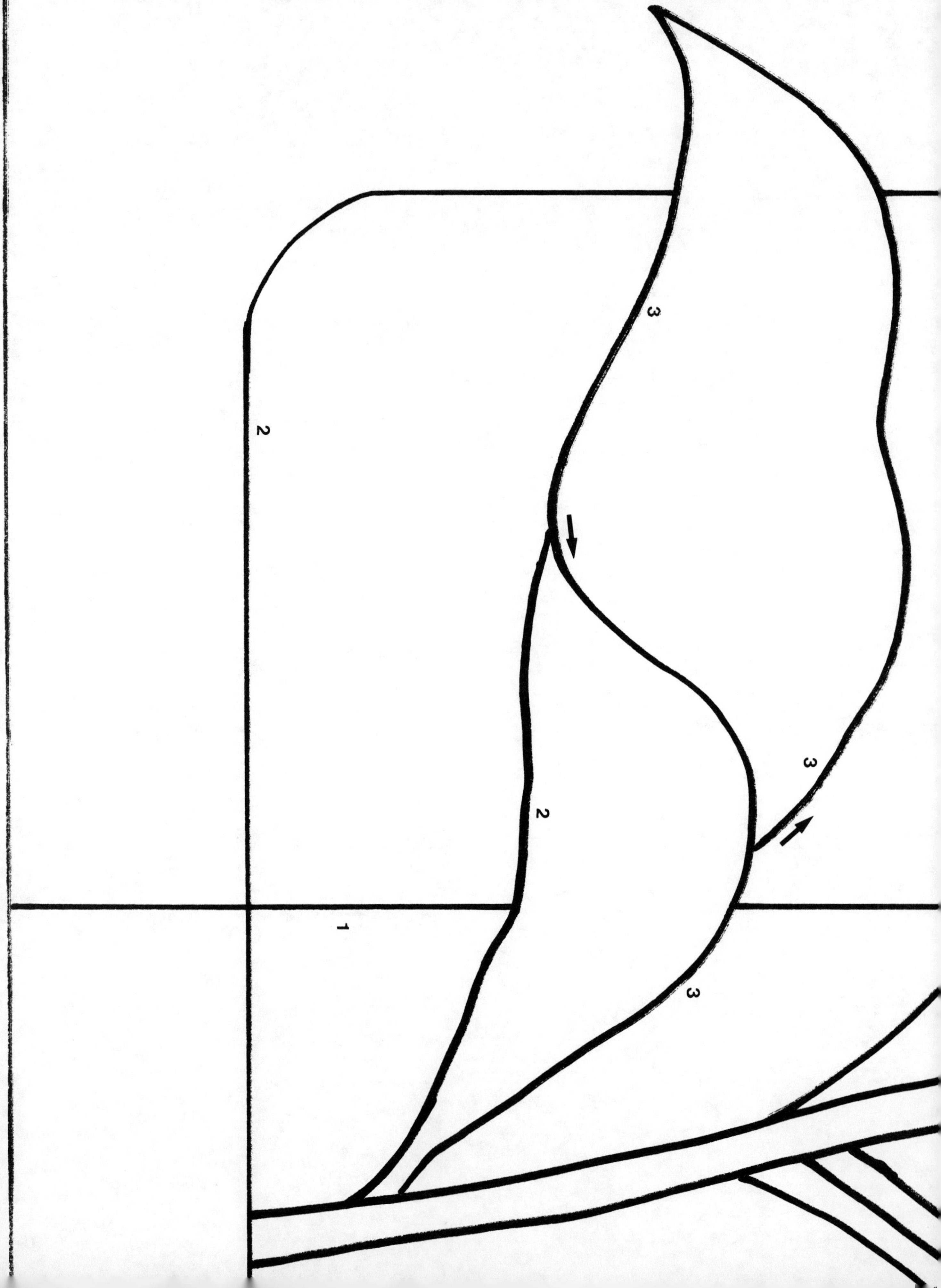
3
2
3
2
1
3

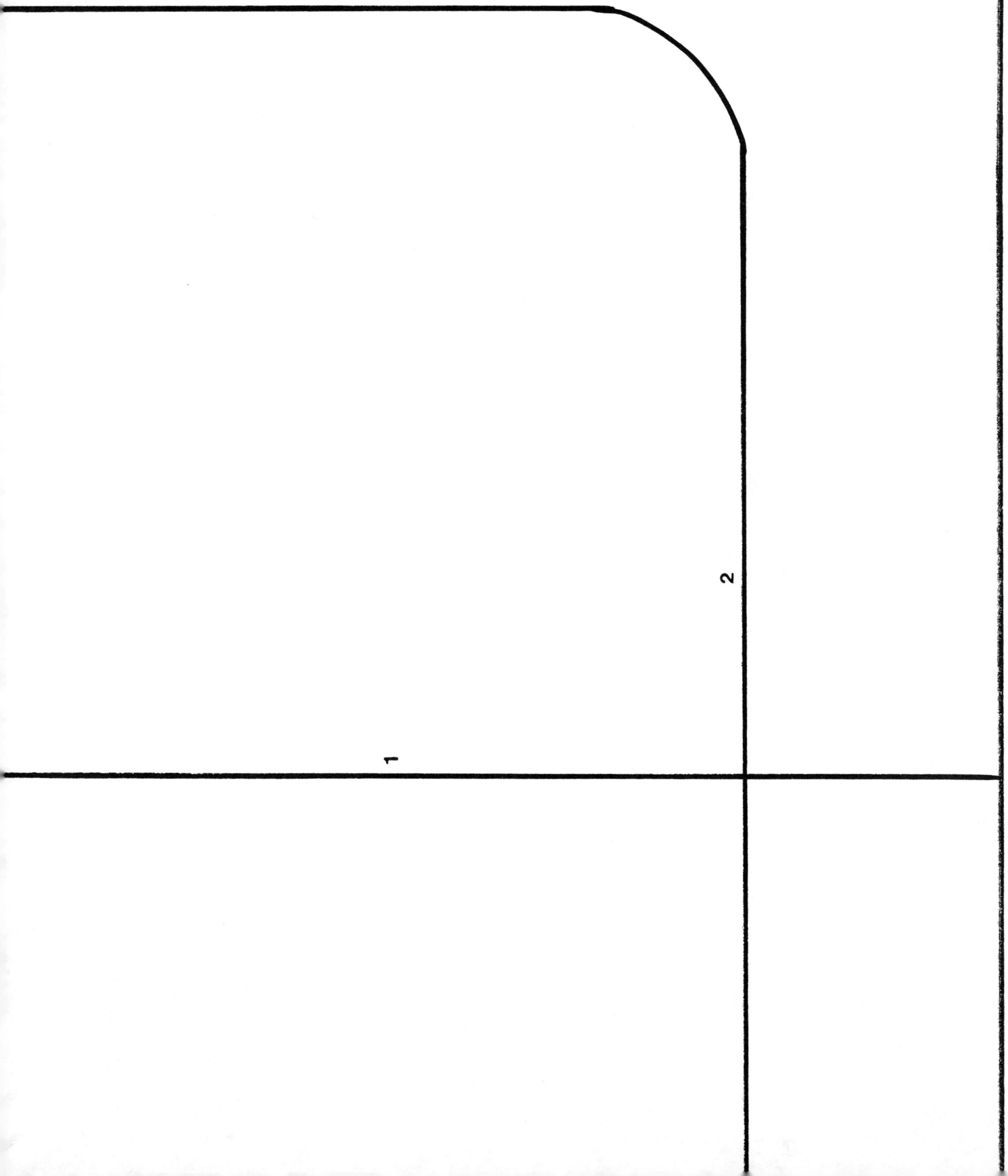
1
2

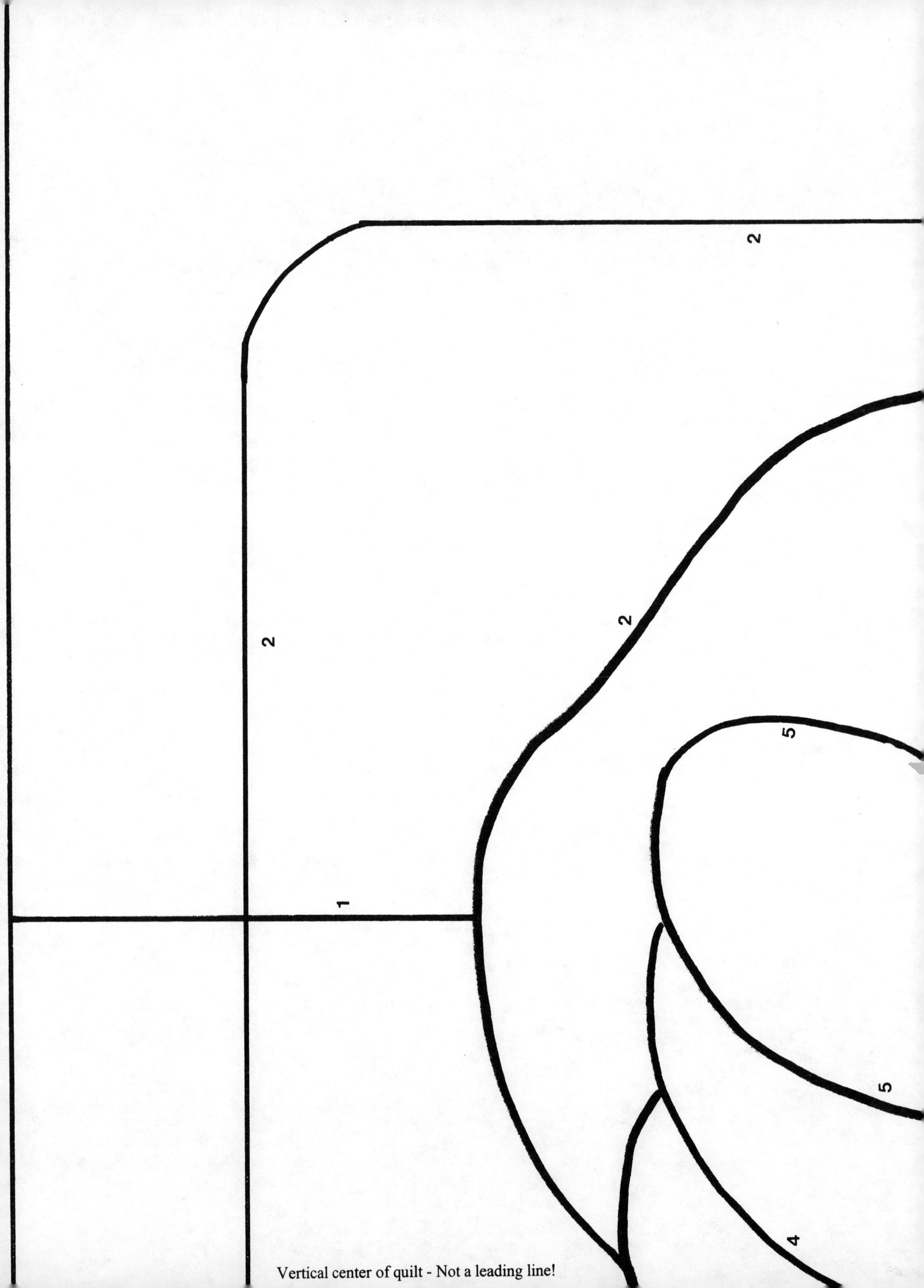
2
2
2
5
1
5
4
Vertical center of quilt - Not a leading line!

Tulips

Bear Paw Productions
4015 Iona Circle • Anchorage, AK 99507
(907)349-7873 • Phone & FAX

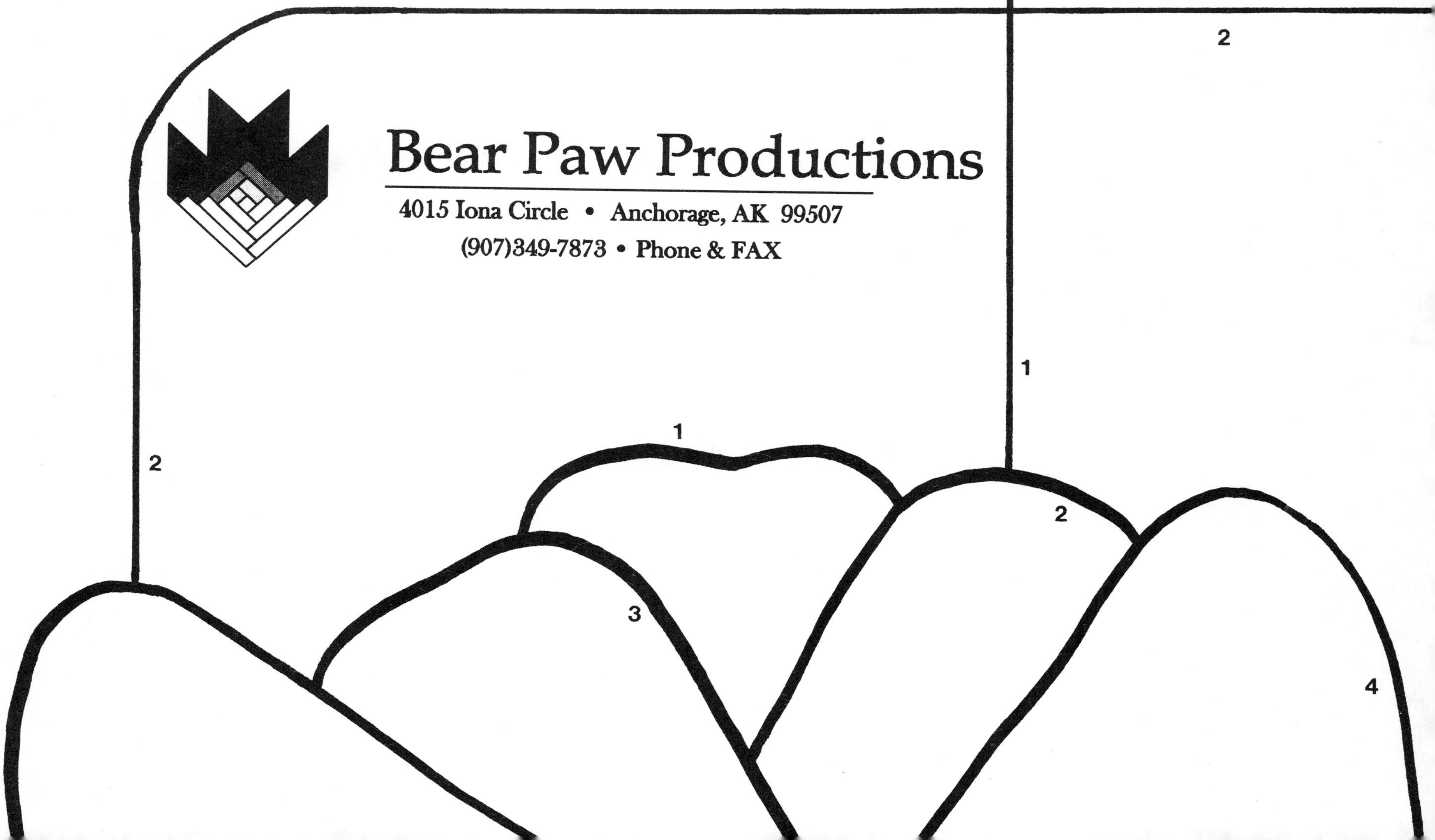

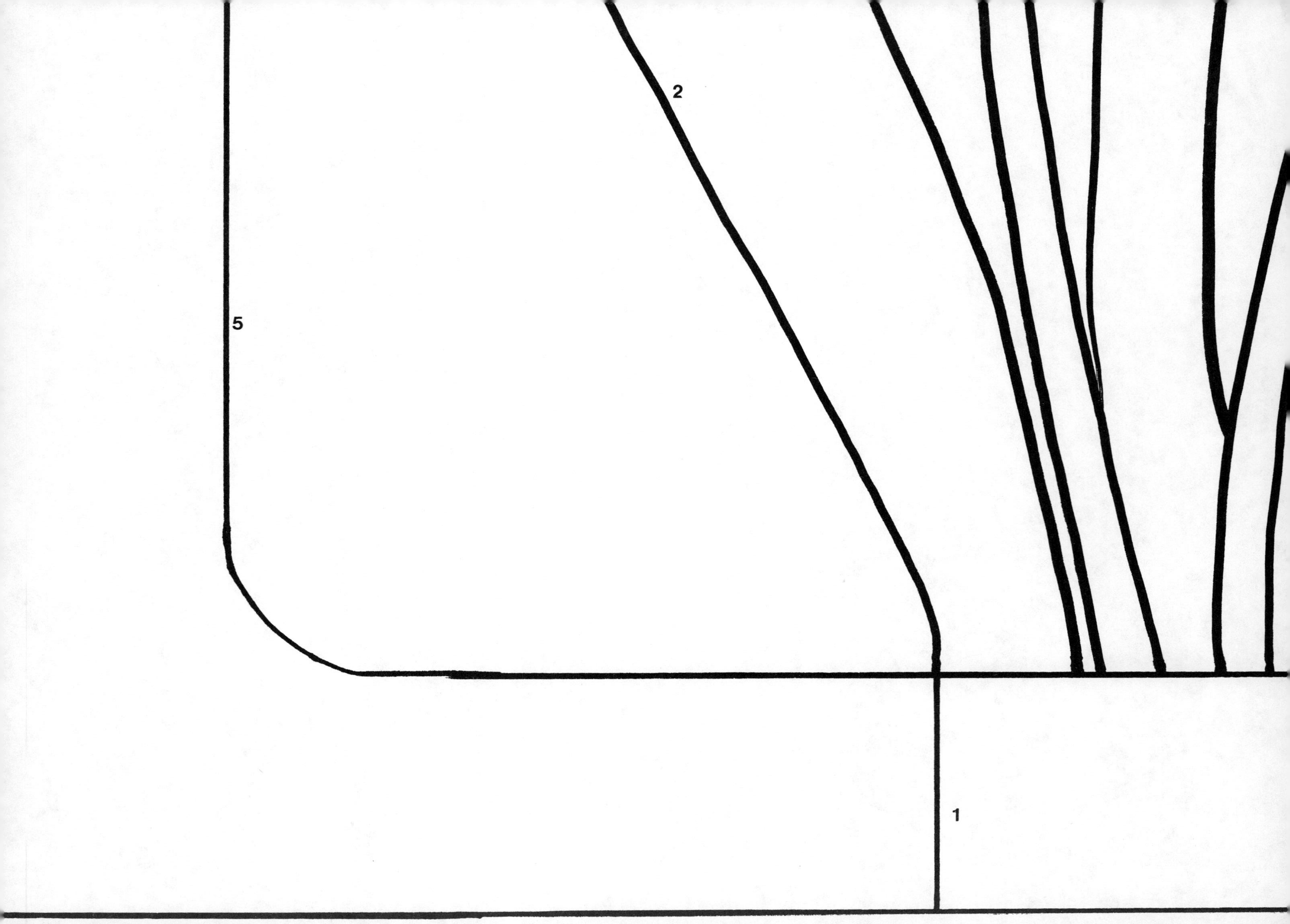
2
5
1

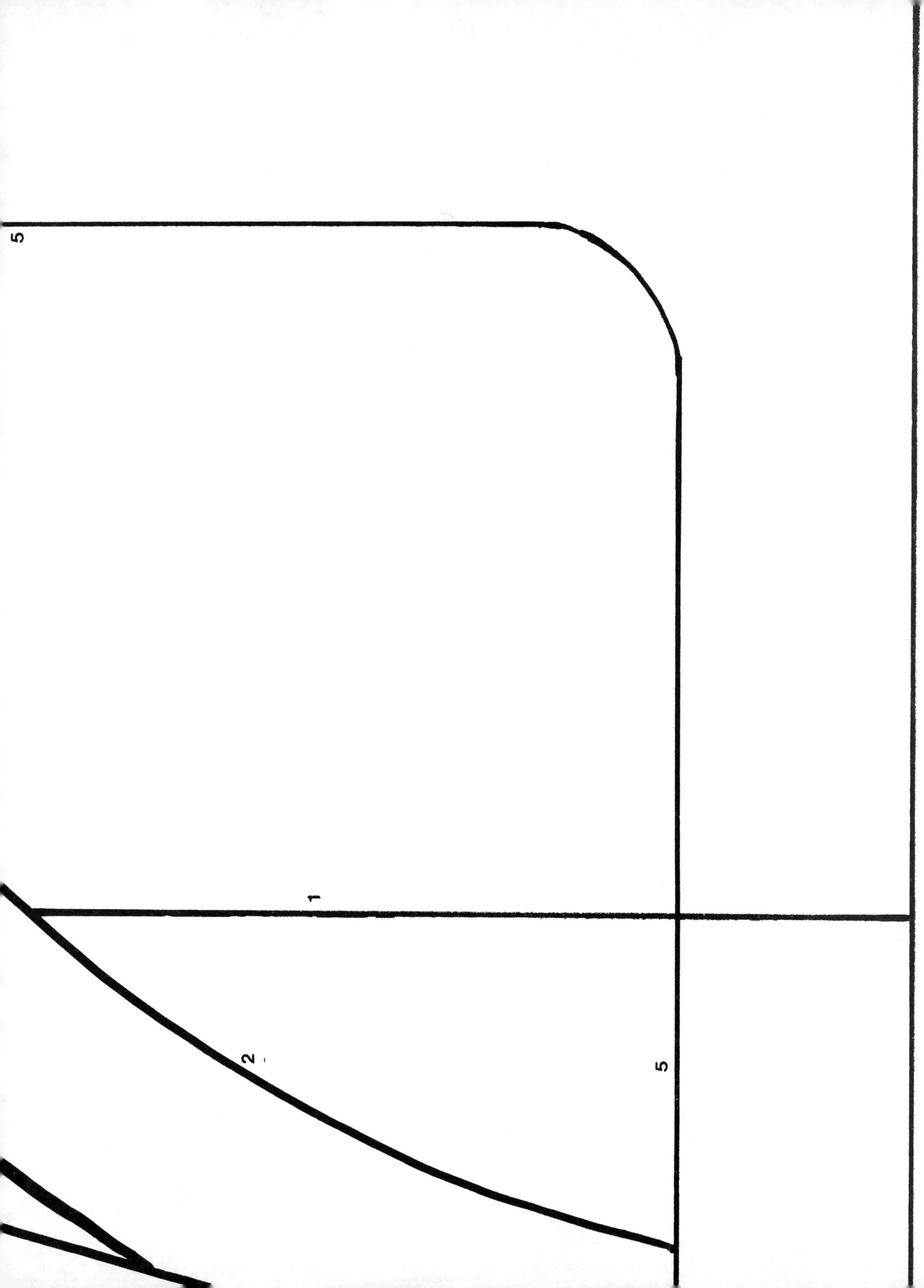
5
1
2
5

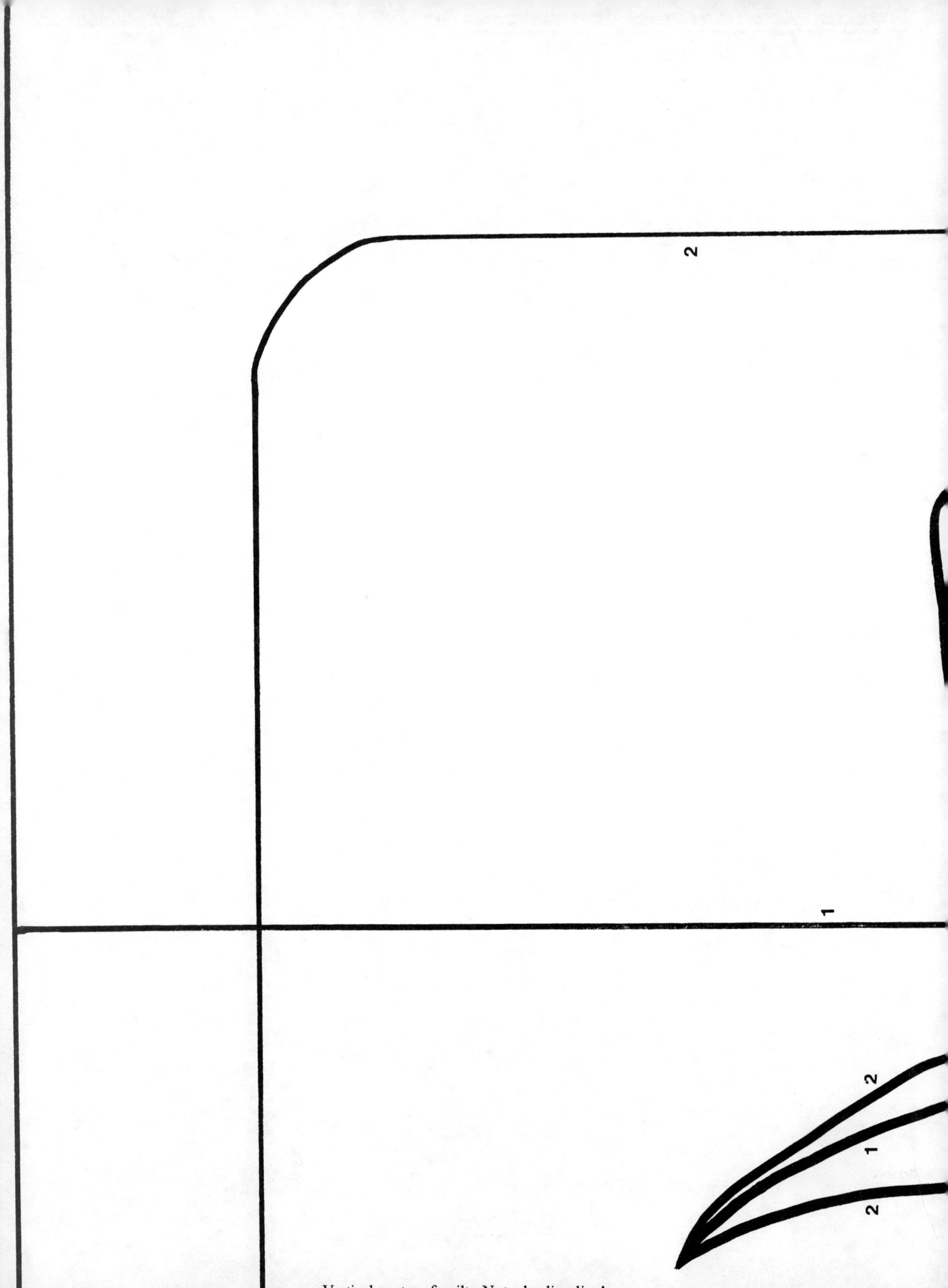

Vertical center of quilt - Not a leading line!

Daffodils

2

Bear Paw Productions
4015 Iona Circle • Anchorage, AK 99507
(907)349-7873 • Phone & FAX

1

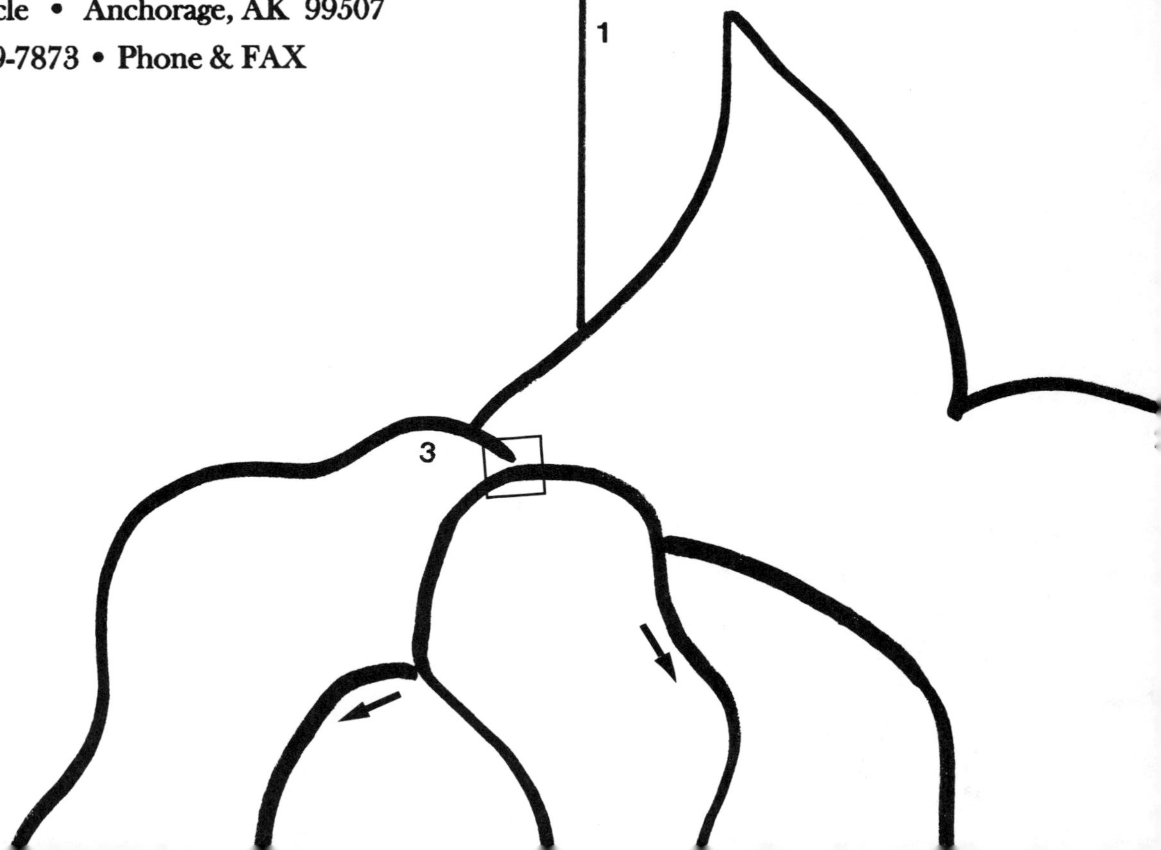

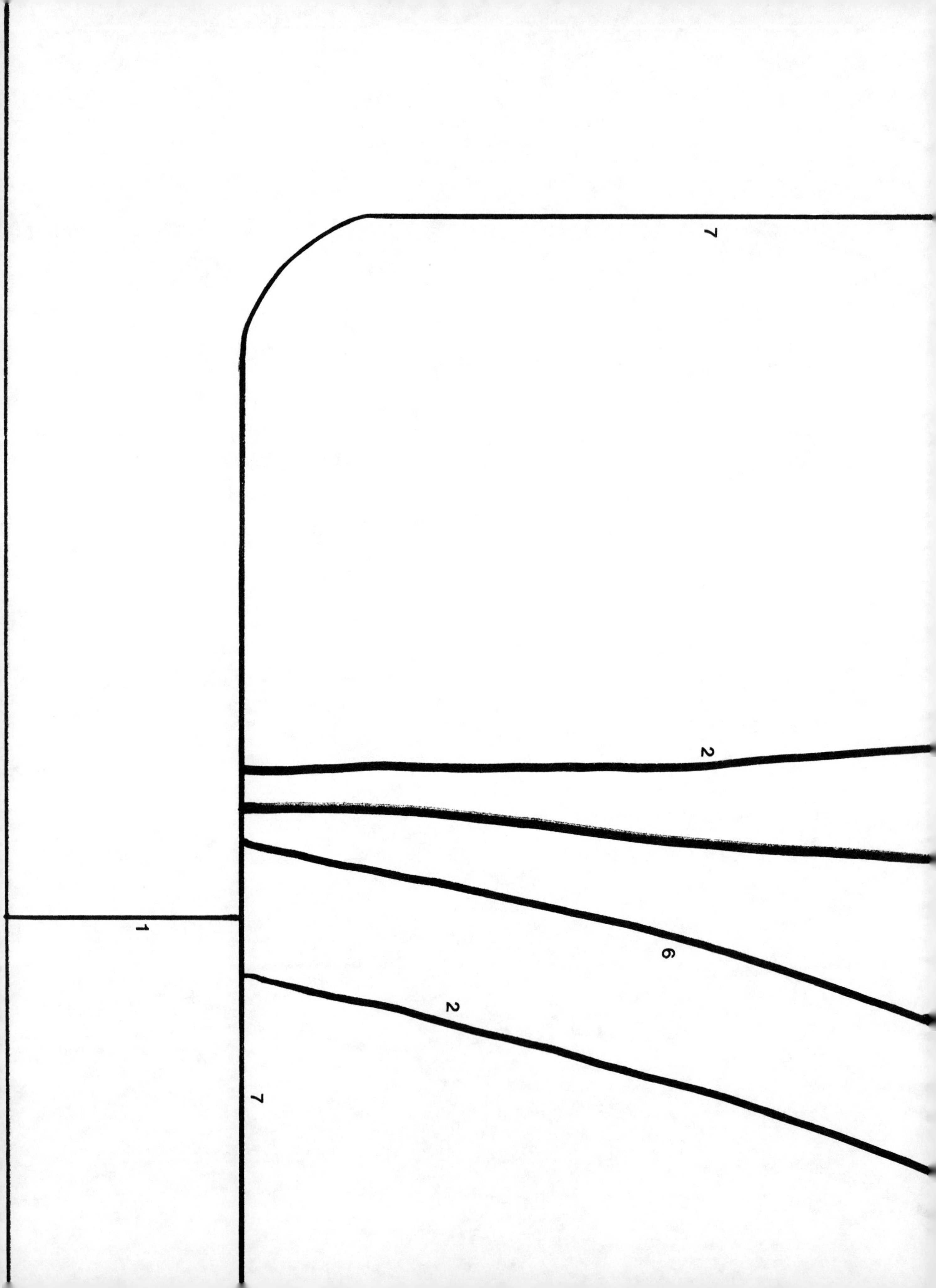
7
2
6
2
1
7

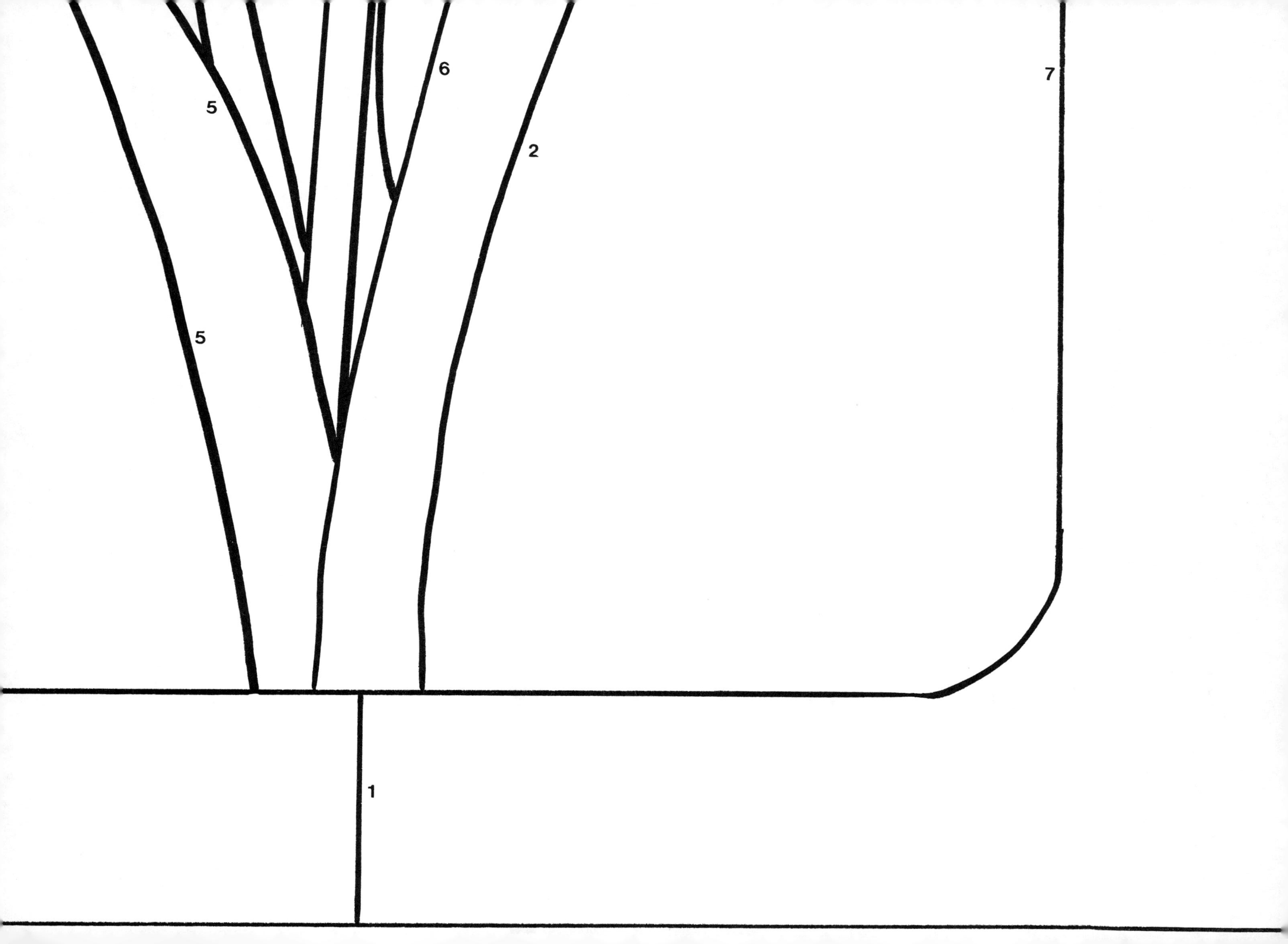
6
7
5
2
5
1

Vertical center of quilt - Not a leading line!

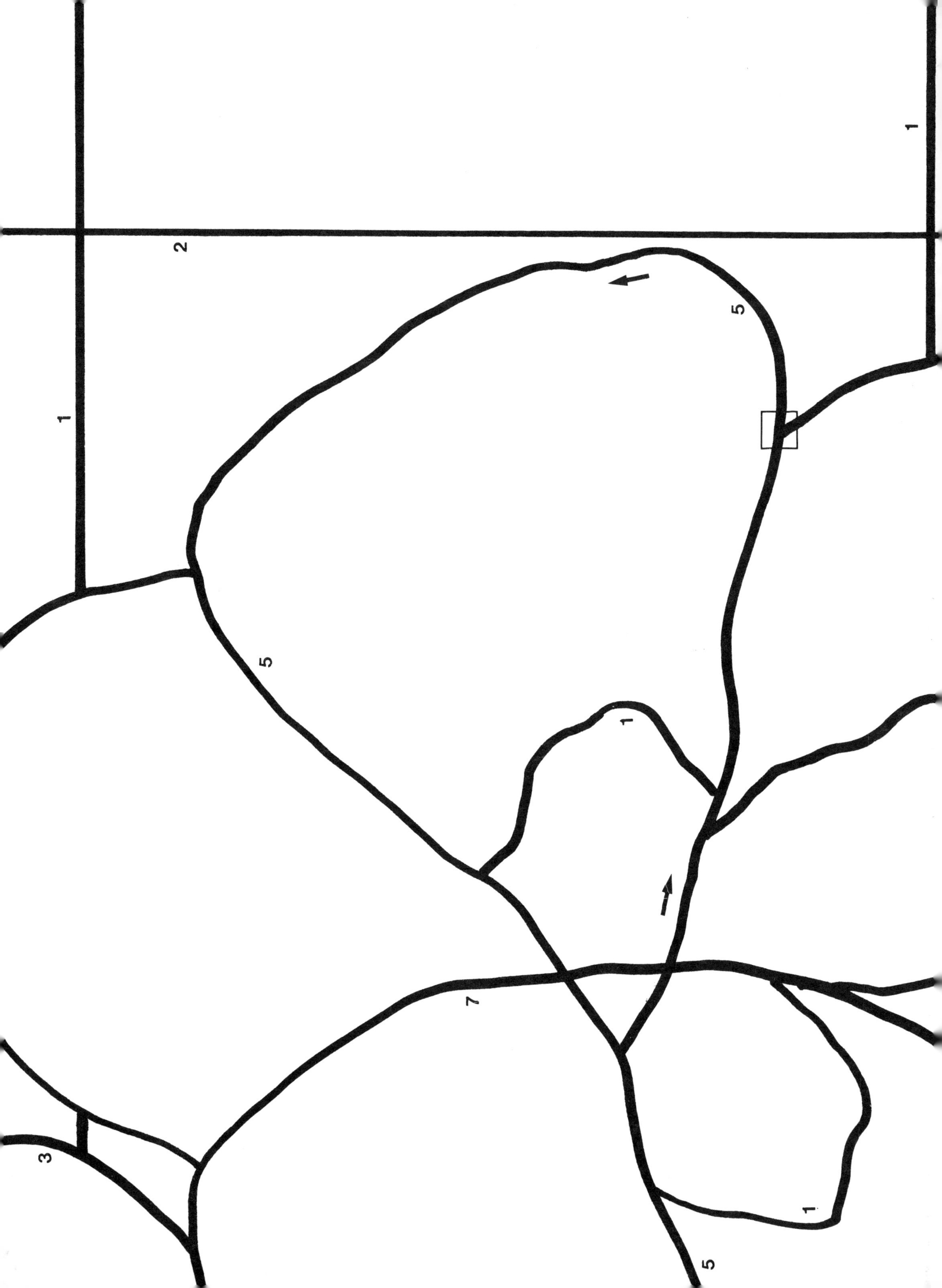
1
2
1
5
5
1
7
3
1
5

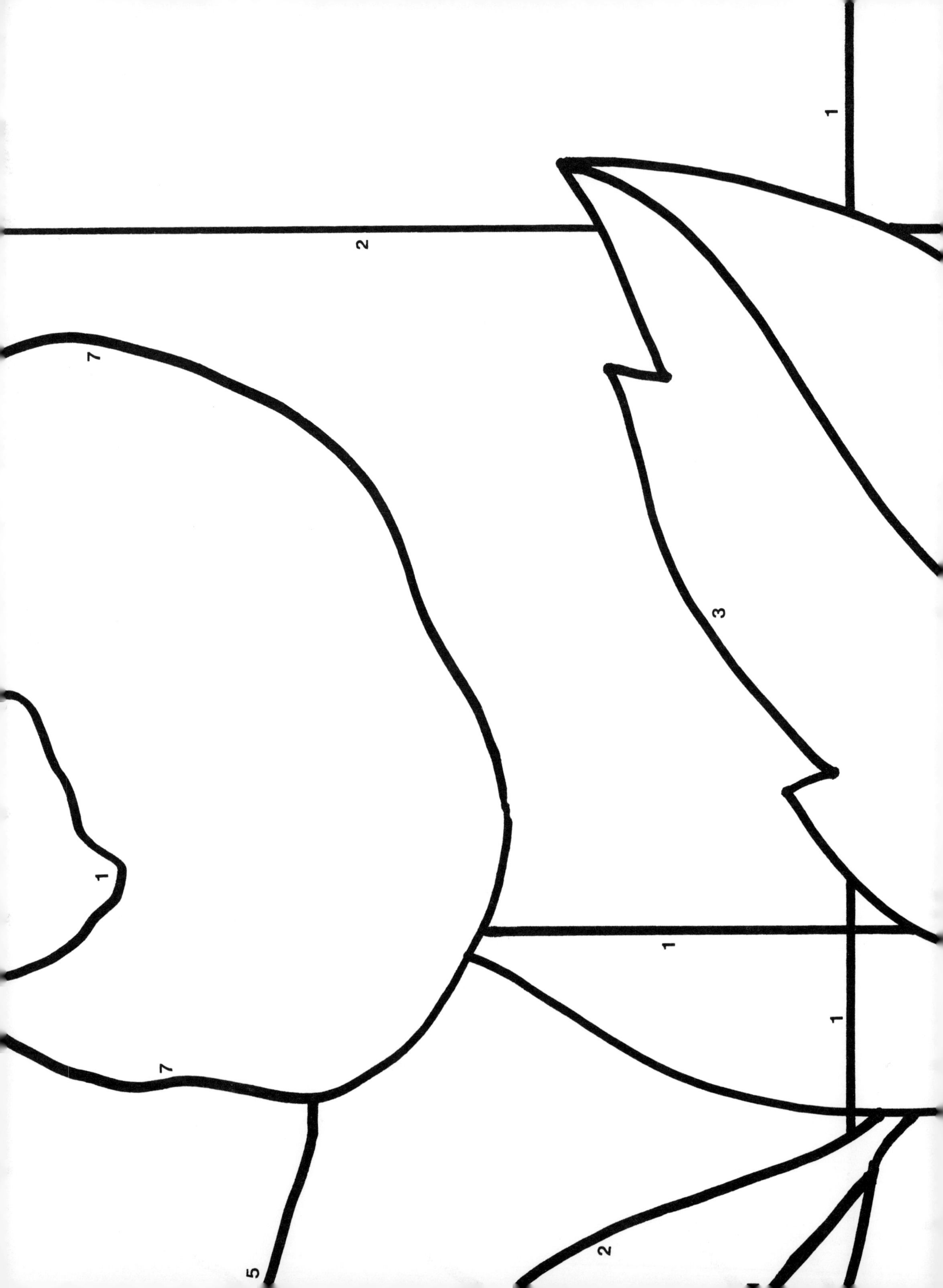
1
2
7
1
3
1
1
7
5
2

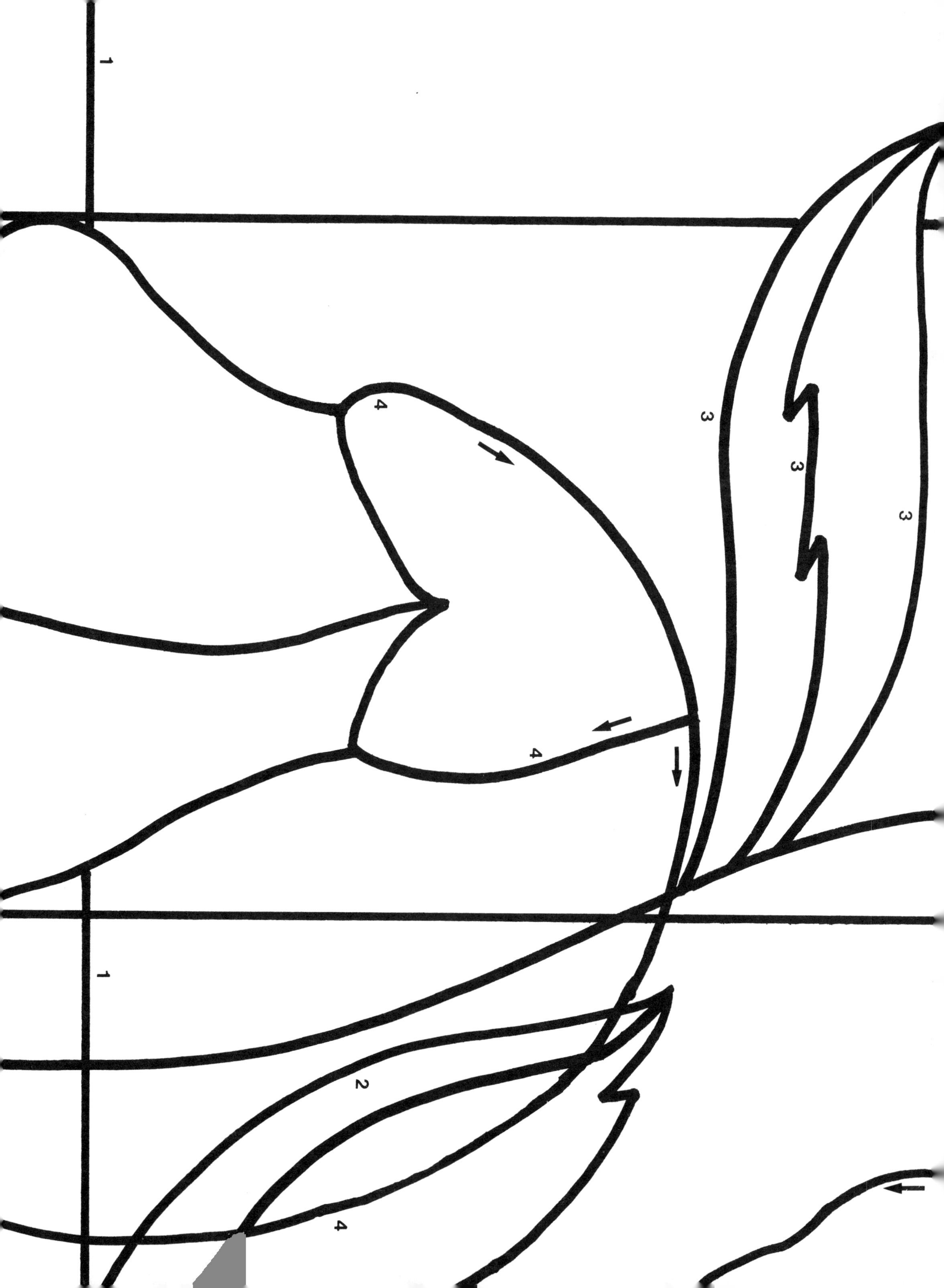
1
4
3
3
3
4
1
2
4

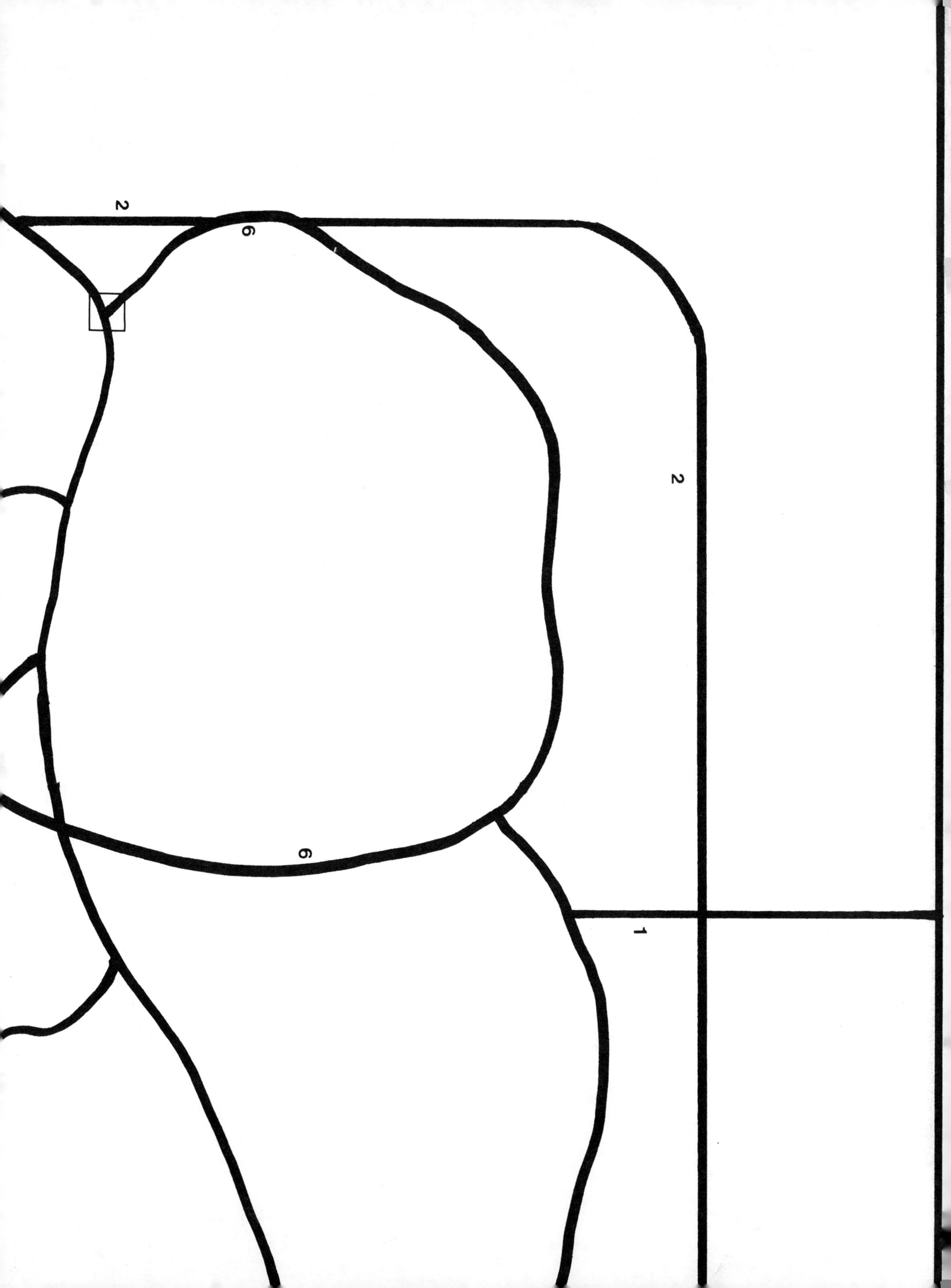
2
6
2
6
1

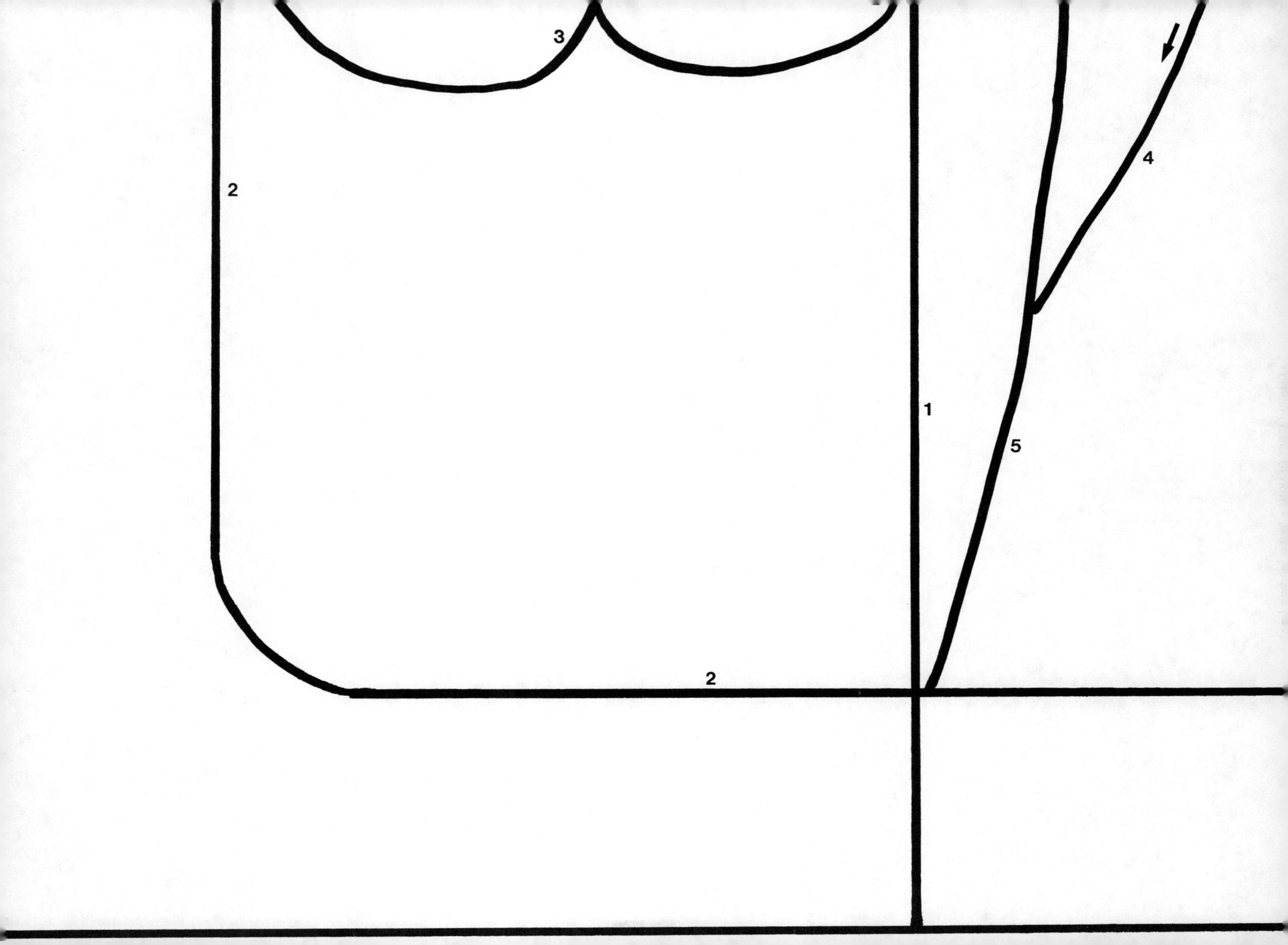
3
4
2
1
5
2

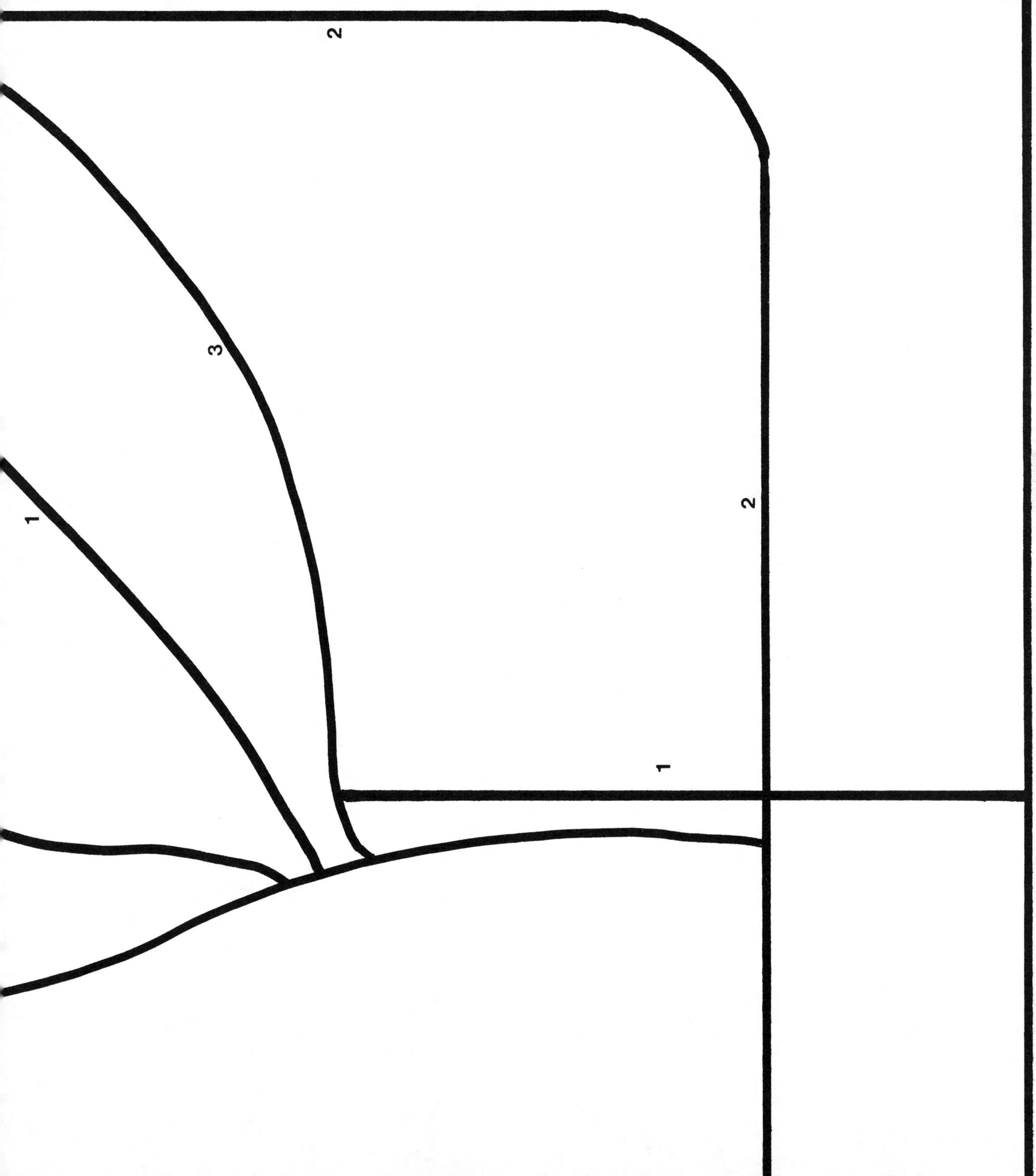

Vertical center of quilt. Not a leading line!

Pansies

2

1

2

Bear Paw Productions
4015 Iona Circle • Anchorage, AK 99507
(907)349-7873 • Phone & FAX

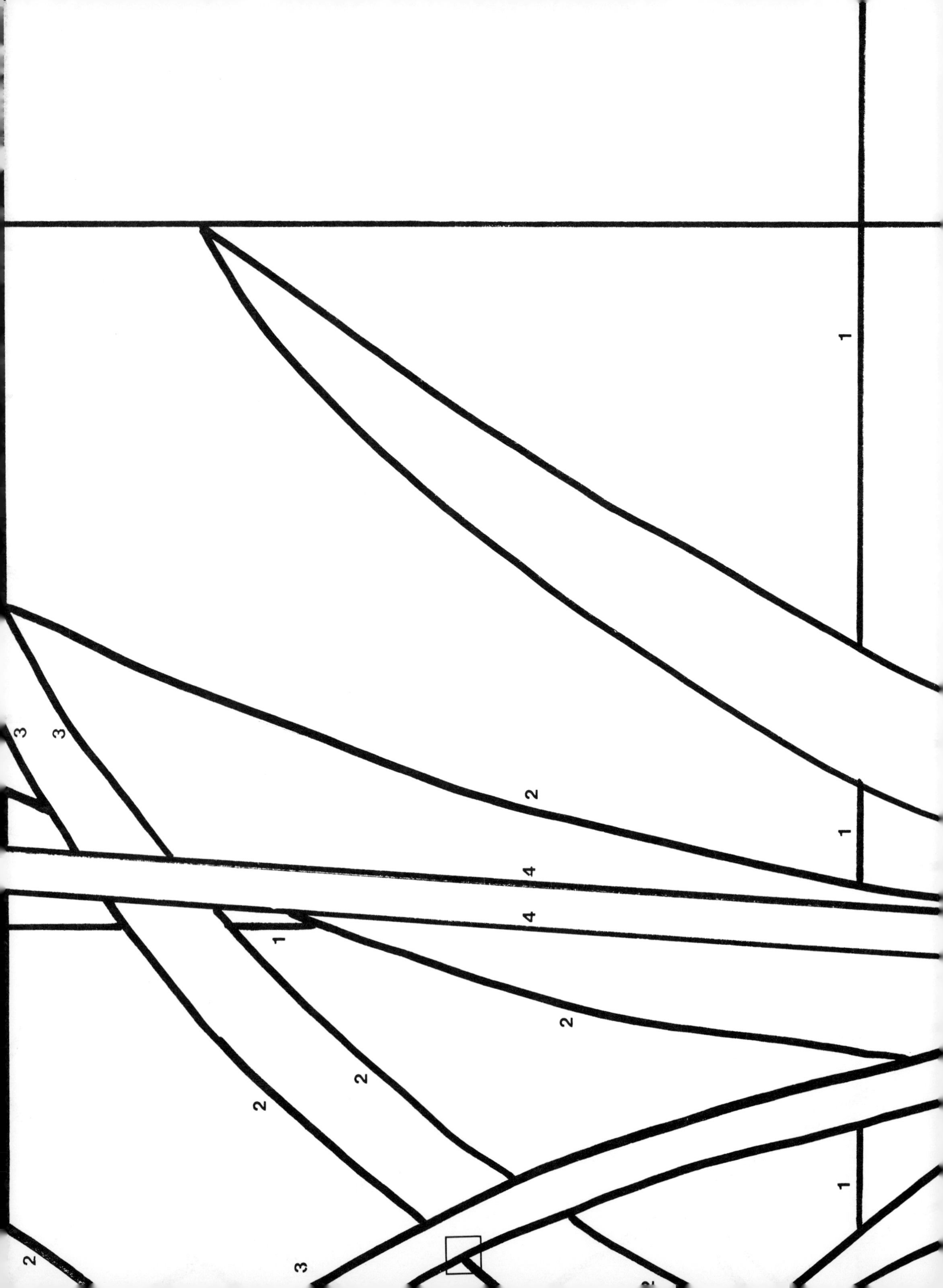
1
3
3
2
1
4
4
1
2
2
2
1
2
3

1
6
6
5
2
3
1
1
5
1
1
2
1

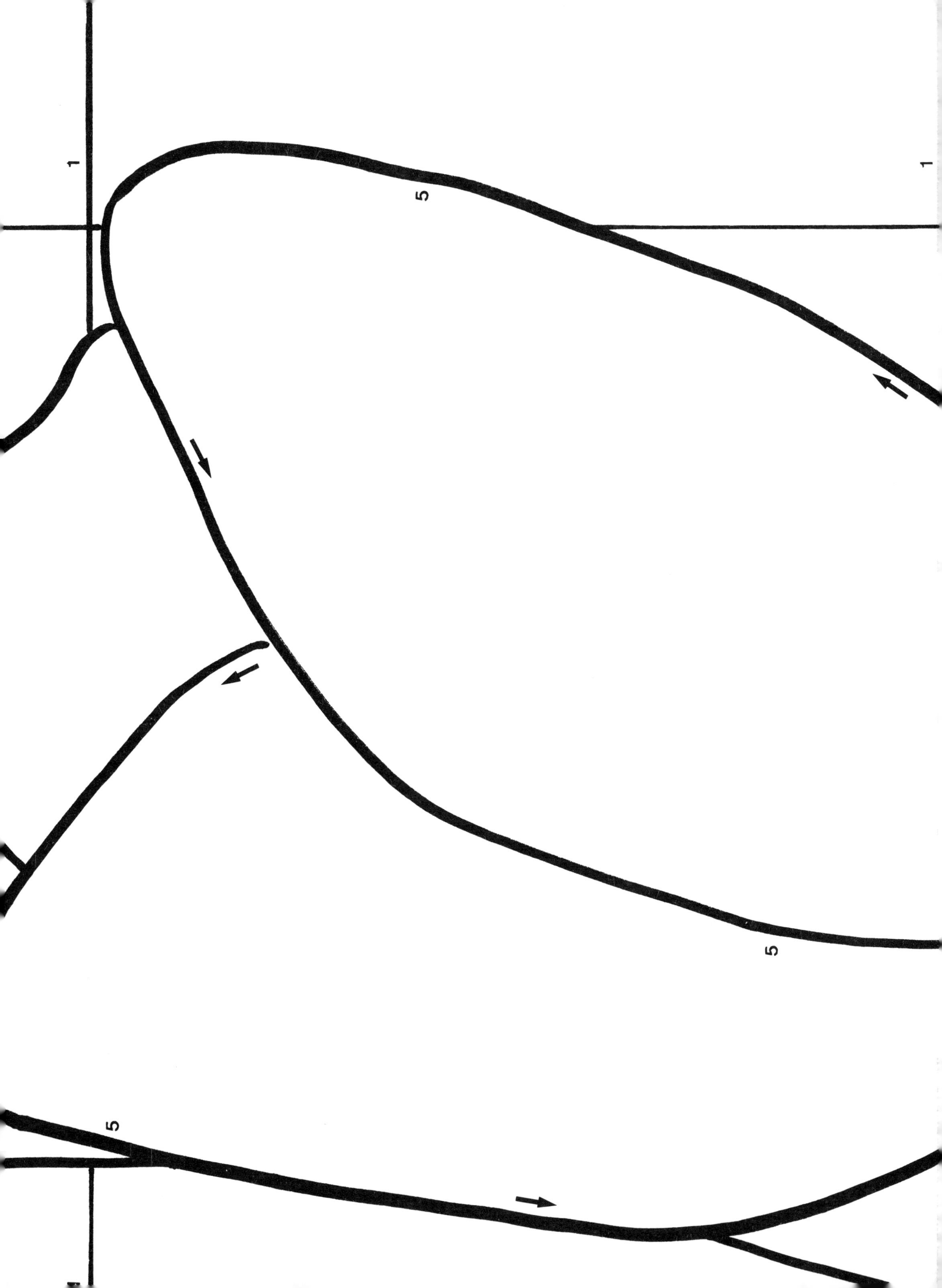
1
5
1
5
5

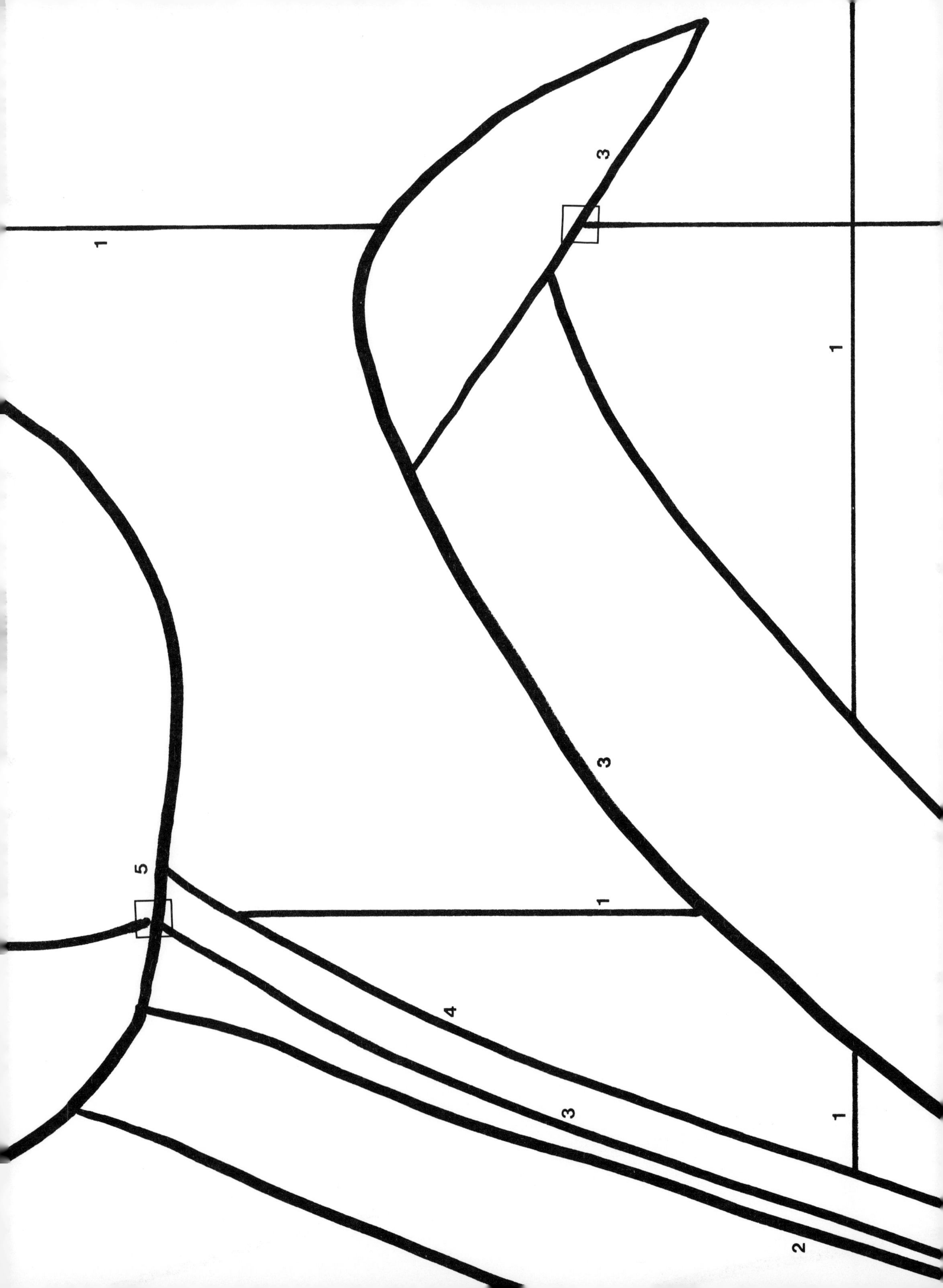
1
3
1
3
5
1
4
3
1
2

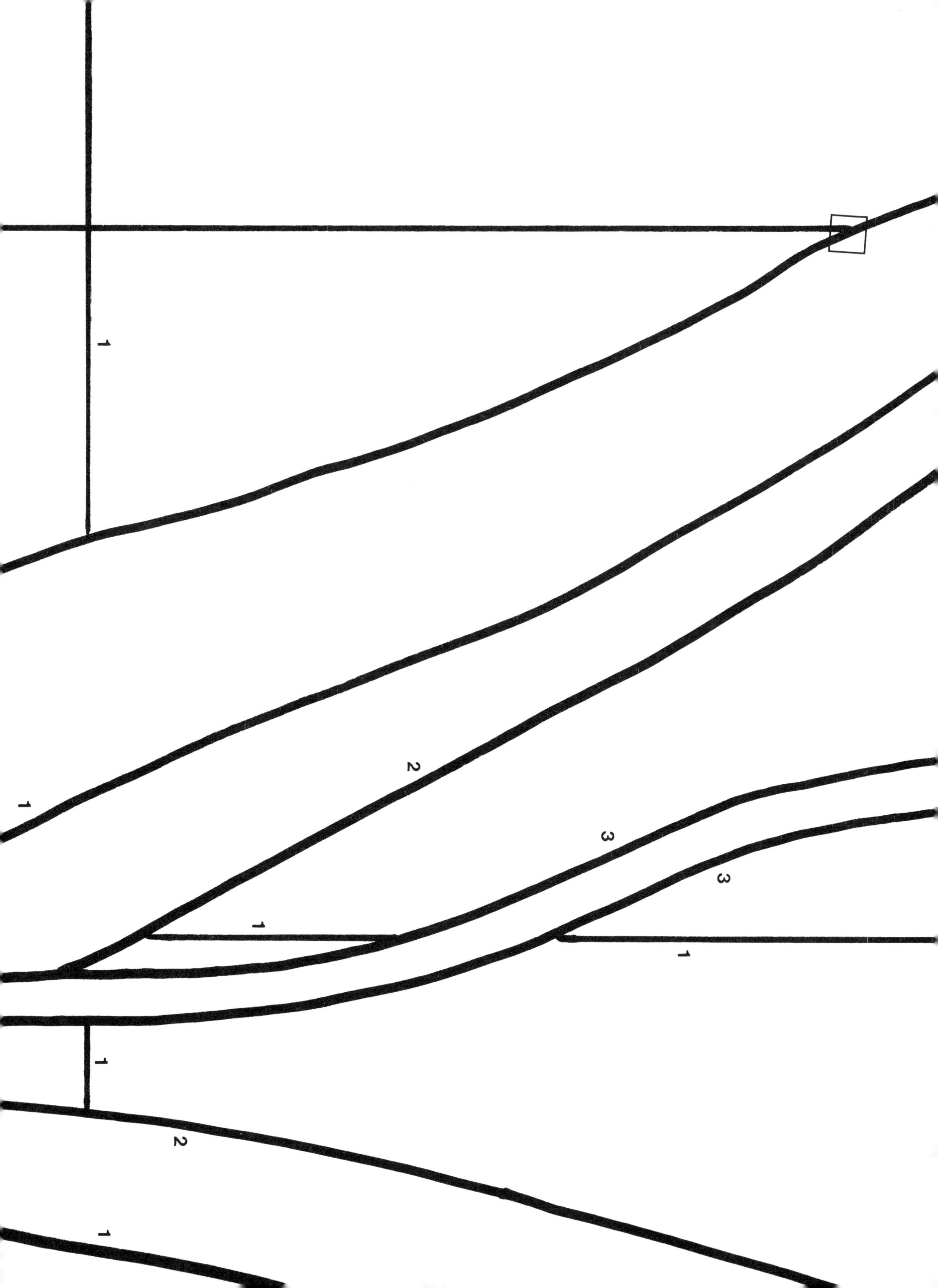
1
1
2
3
3
1
1
1
2
1

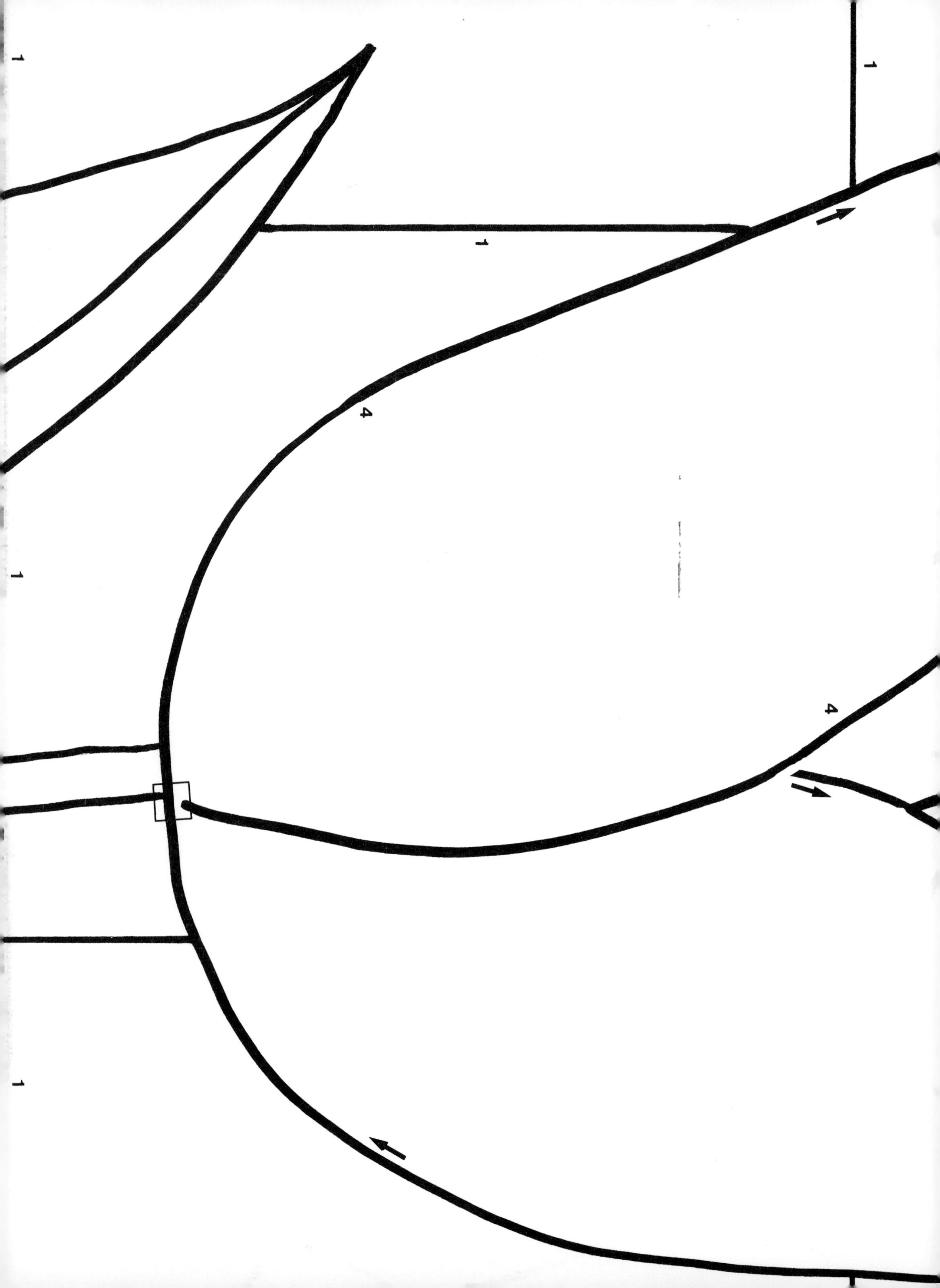
1
1
1
1
1
4
4

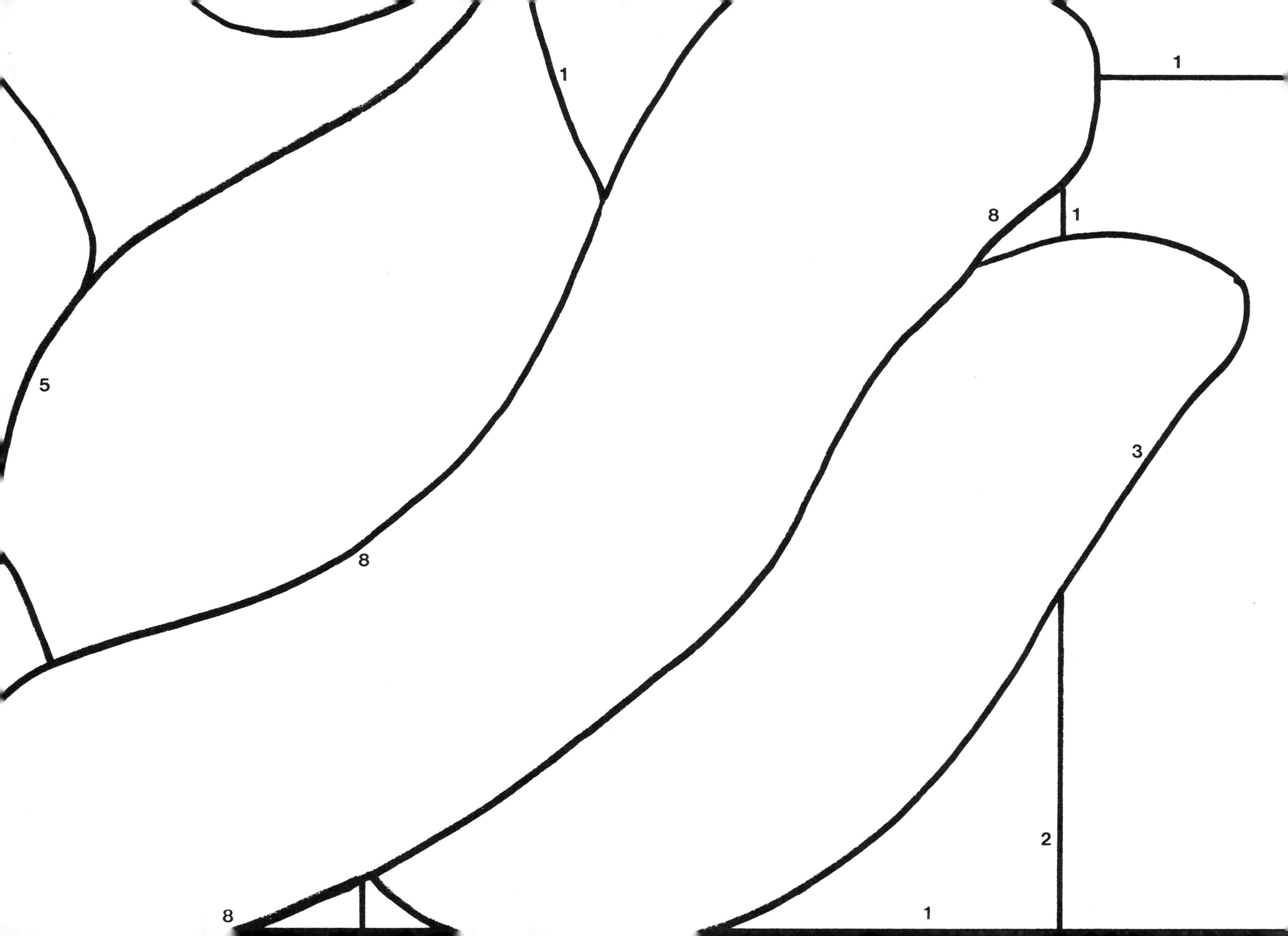
1
1
8
1
5
3
8
2
8
1

2
1
3
4
1
3

2
3
4
1
3
2
3
1
5
5
1
1

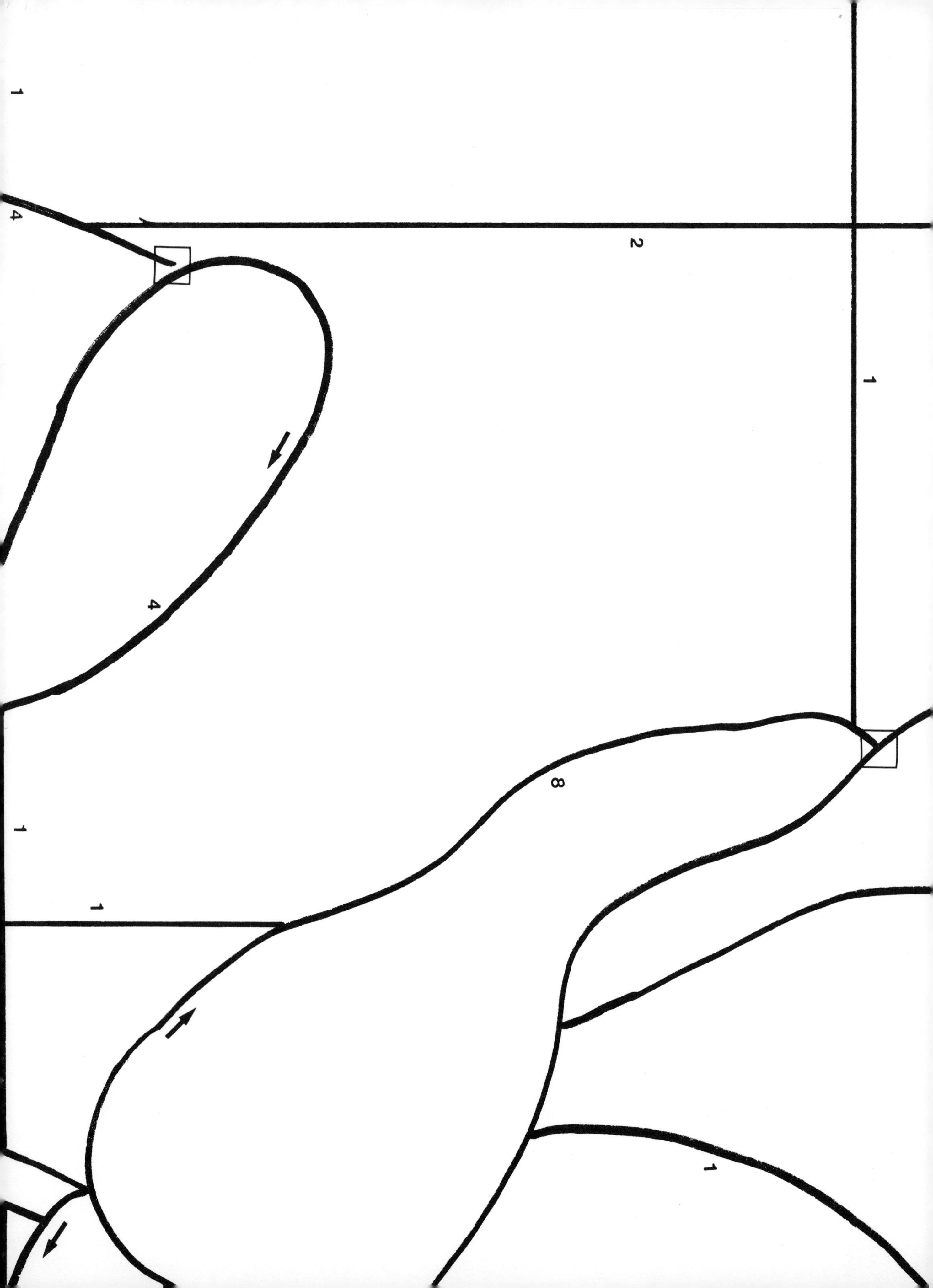
1
4
2
1
4
8
1
1
1

•After glue-basting all fabric pieces to the background, use a pencil to retrace any lines covered by the fabric appliqué pieces that have been cut as one unit - such as lines between the leaf halves.

NOTE: When applying colored fabrics to the background, I generally baste the border segments first. Then I progress to work on the leaves and stems, with the flowers being adhered to the background last. The layers that appear to be toward the back are applied first, the "closer" layers are applied last.

NOTE: Because of the number of pieces involved, I work on the project one flower at a time to avoid confusion; I do not like to reassemble the puzzles created by cutting multiple flowers at one time. Each flower is cut from the freezer paper only when I am ready to work with it - this prevents template pieces from being mislaid or lost.

Bias Tape Application

•The bias tape used in this project is a Clover product. This specific bias tape is used for a number of reasons:

1) **Fusible web** has been applied to the wrong side of the bias tape, allowing all of the bias tape to be pressed in place onto the project before stitching begins.
2) It is slightly narrower than the standard bias tape available and very flexible, allowing tight curves to be negotiated.
3) The fusible web allows the bias tape to be gently pulled from the design and repositioned for the desired results.

•**Clover Quick Bias** is packaged 11 yards per spool.

NOTE: When using the **metallic** fusible bias tape, lower the temperature of your iron. This will lessen the possibility of damage to the bias tape caused by excess heat.

•The bias tape yardages listed for each pattern are slightly larger than the actual amount used when creating the sample quilts. I would recommend starting your first quilt with 2 full spools of bias tape.

•The purpose of the bias tape is to cover the raw edges of all fabric pieces and to simulate stained glass leading.

•Bias tape will cover all raw edges of the appliqué. The bias tape is centered directly over the junction of the appliqué raw edges, over a single raw edge or over the drawn leading line.

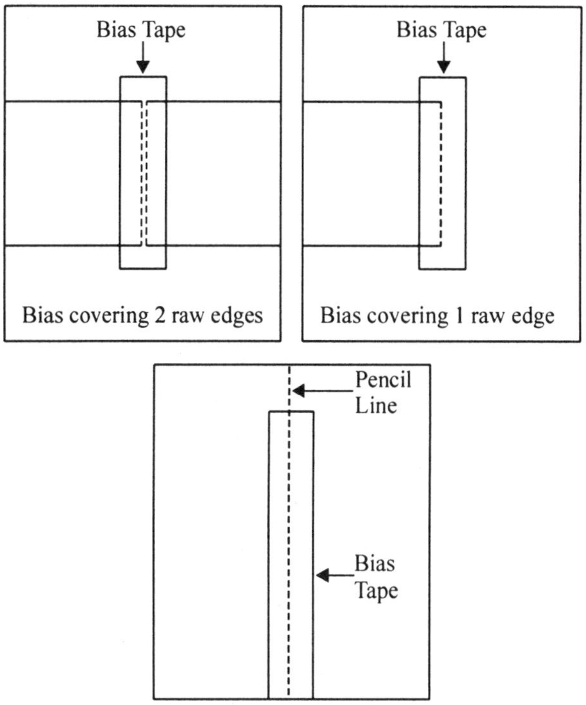

The Bias Tape Numbering System

has been established to help you place bias tape in sequential order. This numbering system ensures that all bias tape raw ends are covered. All pieces will not have a unique number in the sequence. Rather, there will be multiple pieces marked #1, etc.

•Lead all lines marked #1 first. Bias tape lengths marked #1 do not cover the raw end of any other piece of bias tape! All #1 pieces can be fused without disturbing the order of any other pieces.

•Next, place all #2's. These cover the raw ends of #1's.

•Then, place all #3's. These will cover the raw ends of #1's and/or #2's.

•The only place that a raw edge - bias tape or fabric - is allowed, is at the very outer edge of the quilt. This will be encased in the quilt binding!

•Points - Miter the bias tape at each point. Press the fusible bias tape into place up to the point. Insert a pin into the edge of the bias tape where the point of the miter will be positioned. Pull the bias tape against this pin as you fold under the excess fabric, causing the mitered angle to form. In the case of a very sharp point the fold may lay along the outer edge of the bias tape as shown below.

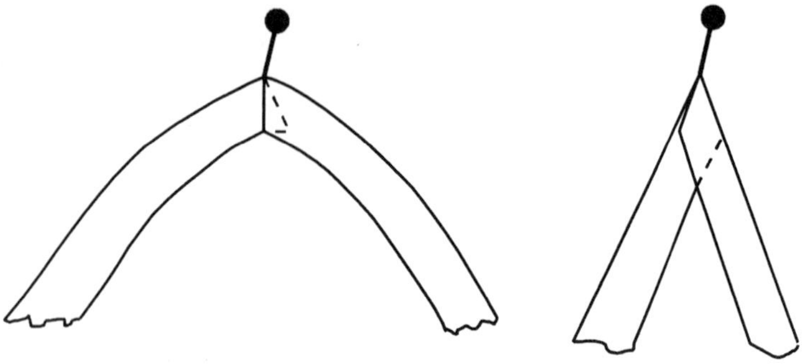

•If you find that you have accidentally applied a piece of bias tape before its time, carefully pull the bias tape away from the appliqué to release just enough space to insert the next bias tape end. You may use a pin to lift the prematurely-placed bias tape from the design. Heating the area a little with the tip of your iron may make the loosening process easier.

•The pattern may include bias tape intersections that are diagramed enclosed by a small box. The box indicates that the first piece of bias tape applied will need to be released from the design and another piece of bias tape inserted. Occasionally this cannot be avoided. Heat may be applied to the bias tape to make it easier to lift.

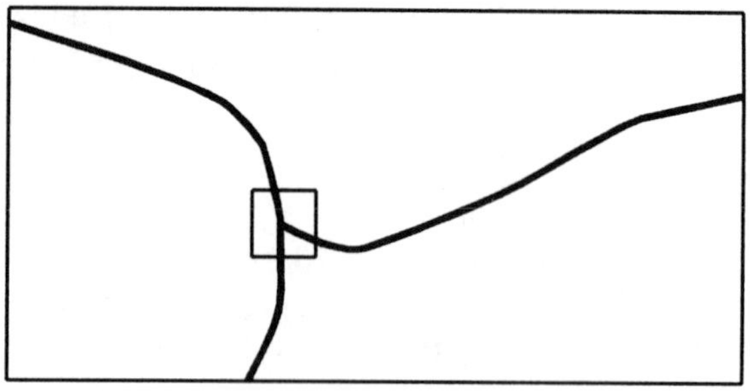

•Trim the end of the bias tape along the leading line that is intersected. This will allow the raw end of the bias tape to be covered (overlapped 1/8") by the next piece of bias tape. This may mean trimming the end of the bias tape at an unusual angle to accommodate the leading line.

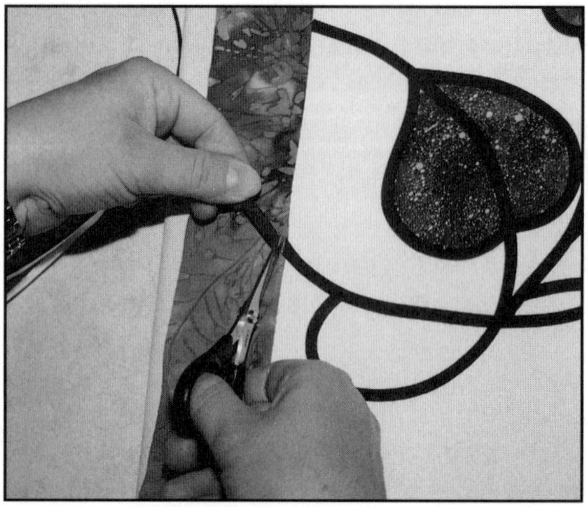

•If you have positioned a piece of bias tape poorly, simply lift it from its place, reposition it, and press it in place with a warm iron.

Woven Fusible Interfacing
Optional

•After all bias tape is pressed in place, adhere a length of woven fusible interfacing to the wrong side of the background fabric, following manufacturers directions. I use only 100% cotton woven fusible interfacing for the best results.

This step is optional! The interfacing gives the quilt top added stability and firmness. This prevents the quilt from "buckling" when the bias tape has been stitched. It also eliminates the need for additional quilting.

Layering the Project

•Layer the quilt with batting and backing.

•Cotton batting works best. The cotton fibers of the batting grip the quilt top and backing. This helps to prevent shifting and puckering.

•The backing and bobbin thread should match the color of the bias tape. If selected in such a manner, the bobbin thread will be unobtrusive on the quilt back. If the bobbin thread should happen to pop to the surface of the quilt it will not be noticeable.

•Baste the layers together using safety pins. Quilt basting spray also works. I have used Sulky® KK 2000 Temporary Spray Adhesive with good results.

Stitching Bias Tape In Place

•Insert a very fine needle into the sewing machine; size 60/8 works well. The holes left by the needle are very small, preventing the bobbin thread from popping to the surface.

•Thread the sewing machine needle with a fine gauge thread to match the color of the bias tape.

Bias Tape	**Thread Choices**
Black	Black Sew Bob (fine lingerie thread)
	Smoke Nylon Thread .004mm

•The bobbin thread may be cotton in a color to match the bias tape.

•Use an open toe embroidery foot on your sewing machine, if you have one. It will be easier to see what you are doing.

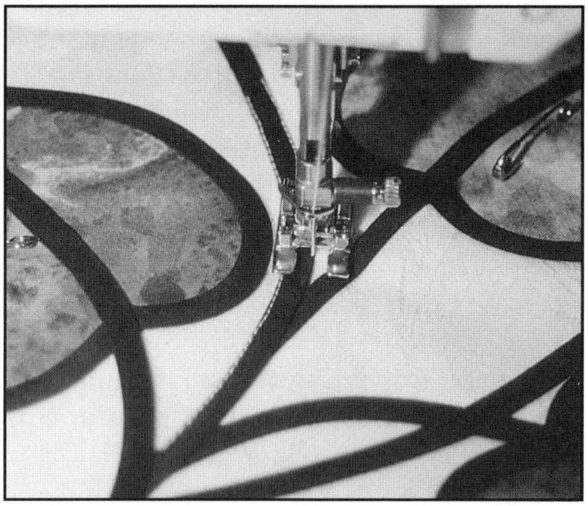

•Stitch both sides of the bias tape in place using a straight stitch. Back stitch at both ends to secure the seam. Stitch at the very edge of the bias tape to avoid an unsightly pleat of bias tape that is not secured. Either side may be stitched first.

•Clip threads close to the surface - front and back of the quilt.

•Use a sewing awl to adjust and smooth bias tape if any puckering has occurred at tight curves.

•If any bias tape should loosen as you are working, it can be secured again by gently pressing it back in place.

Binding

•After all bias tape segments have been sewn, trim the completed quilt along the outer edge of the design.

•Cut 4 strips 2 1/2" wide of binding fabric. Make cut selvedge to selvedge. Stitch strips together on the diagonal as diagramed below. Trim seams to 1/4" and press open.

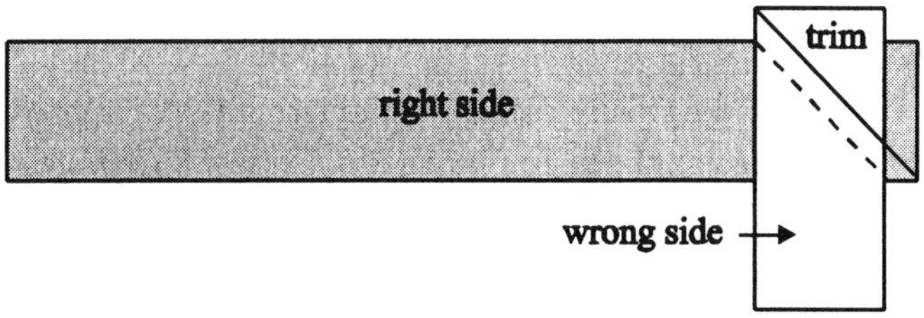

•Press the strip in half lengthwise, wrong sides together.

•Position the folded binding strip so that its lengthwise raw edges are even with the raw edge of the quilt top. Leave 8" free, and begin stitching the binding to the quilt a few inches beyond the center of one edge. Stitch with a 3/8" seam allowance; back tack to secure the seam. Stop stitching 3/8" from the edge and back tack. Remove the quilt from the sewing machine, and snip threads. Rotate the quilt to prepare to sew the next edge.

•Fold the binding strip up, away from the quilt, it will fold nicely at a 45° angle. Fold it again to bring the strip edge along the raw edge of the quilt top. This fold should be even with the top edge of the quilt. Begin stitching at the fold, stitch through all layers.

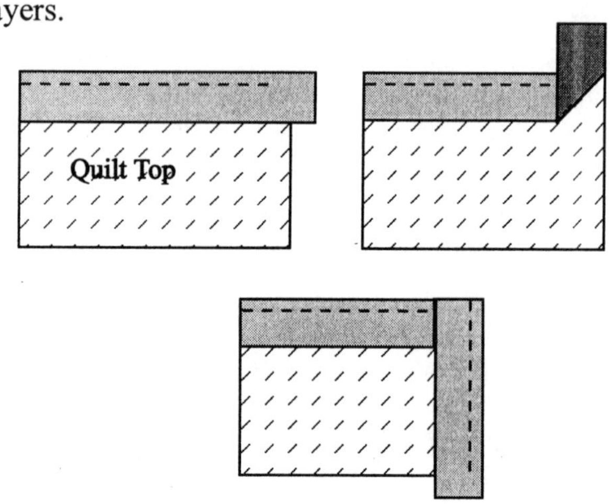

•Continue sewing around the quilt in this manner until you are within 12" of the starting point; back tack.

•To finish the quilt, fold each strip back on itself so that the folds meet in the middle of the 12" gap. Finger press a crease at the folds.

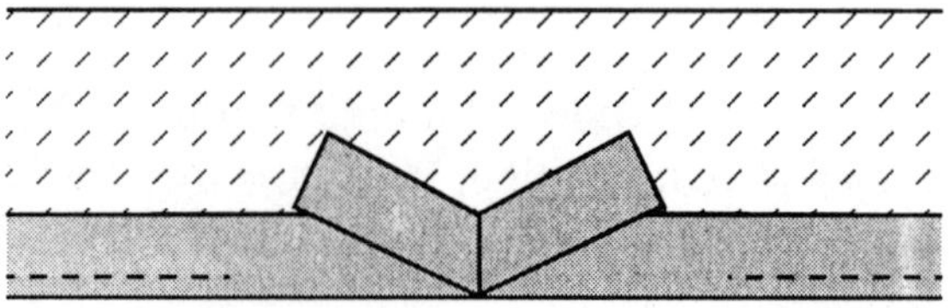

•Trim the excess strip fabric 1 1/4" from both folds.

•Open the folded strips and place the strips right sides together as diagramed below. Fold the quilt out of your way to allow the binding strips to be aligned properly. Stitch the strips together with a diagonal seam. Trim the seam allowance to 1/4" and press the seam open.

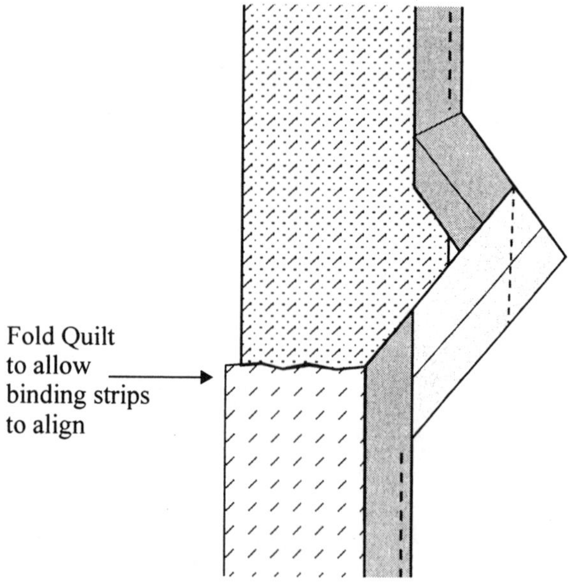

•Fold the binding strip together again and finish stitching the binding strip to the edge of the quilt.

•Hand stitch the folded edge of the binding to the back side of the quilt with a blindstitch. Use a thread that matches the binding. The fold of the binding should just cover the seamline.